VICTORIAN
HOUSE STYLE

**AN ARCHITECTURAL AND INTERIOR
DESIGN SOURCE BOOK**

Conceived and designed by John Strange and
Megra Mitchell

First published 1991
Reprinted 1992 (three times), 1993, 1994 (twice),
1996, 1997 (twice), 1998, 1999

First published in paperback 2001

Conceived, edited and designed by John Strange and
Megra Mitchell
Researchers: Chris Gomes, Charlotte Osborne

A catalogue record for this book is available from the
British Library.

ISBN 0 7153 1319 3 (paperback)

Printed in Singapore
for David & Charles
Brunel House, Newton Abbot, Devon

VICTORIAN
HOUSE STYLE

AN ARCHITECTURAL AND INTERIOR DESIGN SOURCE BOOK

LINDA OSBAND

David & Charles

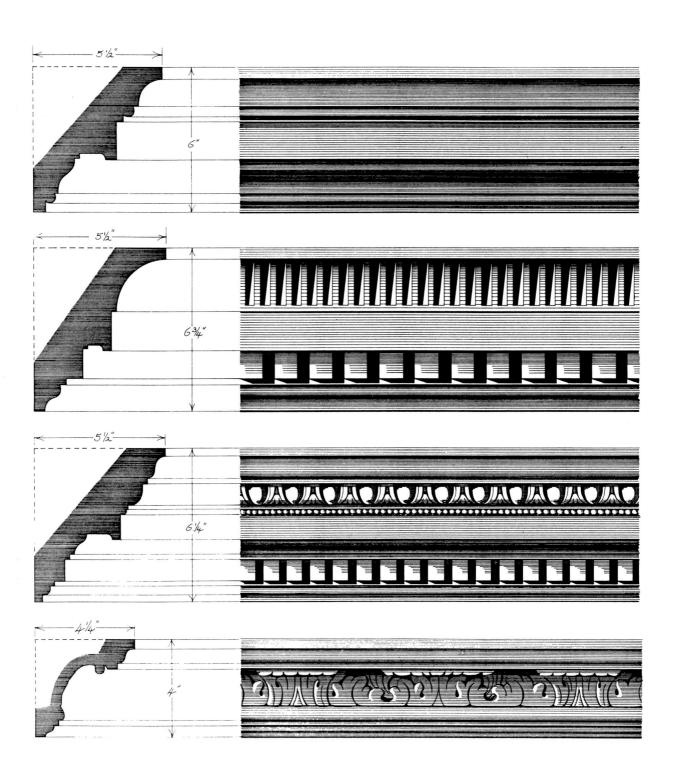

Contents

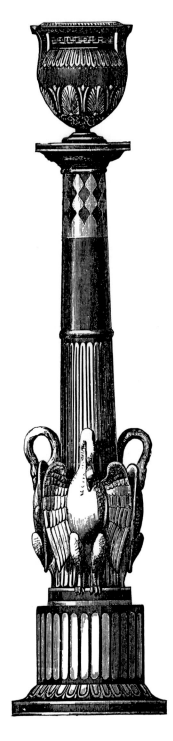
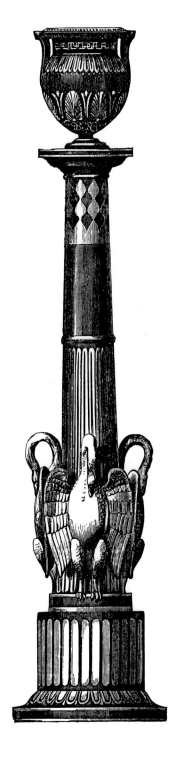

Introduction

Architect: '*you choose the style of your house just as you choose the build of your hat; – you can have classical, either columnar or non-columnar, either arcuated or trabeated, either rural or civil, or indeed palatial; you can have Elizabethan in equal variety; Renaissance ditto; or ... Mediaeval – the Gothic which is now so much the rage – in any one of its multifarious forms ... feudalistic, monastic, scholastic, ecclesiastic, archaeologistic, ecclesiologistic, and so on.* ' *Gentleman Client:* '*But really, I would much rather not. I want a plain, substantial, comfortable Gentleman's House ... I don't want any style at all.*'

Robert Kerr, The Gentleman's House (1864)

Left: The southern transept of the Crystal Palace, the magnificent glass and iron building designed by Joseph Paxton for the Great Exhibition in 1851. **Opposite:** The Gothic Revival movement was one of the many architectural styles battling for prominence in the mid–Victorian era. Its influence can be seen on this house in north London built in 1865.

A selection of products on display at the Great Exhibition. Many of these highly decorated pieces of furniture found their way into the homes of the new monied middle classes, including the sociable' (opposite) and the newly invented gas chandelier.

Queen Victoria ruled from 1837 to 1901, an era in which great social and technological changes occurred, many of which had profound effects on the architectural development of the period. The Industrial Revolution had been under way for almost eighty years, bringing with it dramatic improvements in transportation and the mass production of building materials, while at the same time creating a large, increasingly prosperous, property–owning middle class, who extolled the virtues of family life and who wanted homes which proclaimed to the world their new status and social position.

Easier access to city and industrial centres via the expanding network of roads and railways led to a shift in the population and a rapid mushrooming of new towns and suburbs on the outskirts of most main cities. Whilst the aristocracy retained their country estates and elegant town houses, and the working classes stayed in rural areas or in the overcrowded inner cities, members of the new monied class rushed to the suburbs in order to achieve their dream of owning a house and garden of their own. This not only gave them privacy and a means by which to fulfil their social aspirations, but it also removed them from the health hazards posed by inner–city life, where bad sanitation and slum dwellings helped to spread disease. The subsequent demand for suitable houses, the growth of the suburbs and the virtual doubling of the population resulted in a massive building boom during

Victoria's reign.

Architects had always enjoyed a high position in society, but builders and labourers were usually drawn from its poorer sections. Thomas Cubitt (1788–1855) was the first speculative builder to change this situation. He established a permanent workforce of over a thousand men and made popular the idea of tendering for a job: with one firm being responsible for the entire project instead of each individual being contracted to work on a particular part of it. As a result, he could control the quality of his workforce and his estates became renowned for their high standards of building. He was also one of the first builders to concern himself with the overall facilities on an estate, such as the drainage and sewage arrangements, and the provision of good roads and street lighting. His developments of formal terraced houses, faced with stucco and flanked by imposing classical columns, became a distinctive feature of certain parts of London – for example, Belgravia and Pimlico – and were soon copied in other major cities.

To meet the increasing need for new houses, Victorian speculative builders came into their own. The expansion of suburban life, the growing prosperity of the *nouveaux riches* and the availability of finance provided the speculator with ample opportunity to make a profit. The scale of their operations varied enormously, with some builders constructing only a couple of houses, whilst

entrepreneurs like Cubitt developed large estates. The Public Health Act of 1848 and the Metropolitan Building Act of 1844, plus the new Housing Acts after 1875, led to more control over the standards of house building, with regulations laid down for street plans, drainage, sanitation, the minimum width between buildings, the amount of natural light and ventilation to be supplied, the inclusion of damp–proof courses, the size of windows and height of ceilings, and the quality of workmanship and materials employed. Tax on glass and windows was abolished in 1845 and 1851 respectively, and on bricks in 1850, which resulted in glass and brick becoming cheaper; they were therefore used more frequently, which affected the overall design of buildings in the second half of the century.

Throughout the Victorian era, vast, imposing houses were built in town and country for the aristocracy, and humble terraced houses began to be provided for the poor, but the most revolutionary development was the growth of housing which catered for the middle classes. These homes changed the face of most towns and cities and gave them the character which we know today. They still constitute a large part of the country's housing stock, with the result that many of their present inhabitants are now occupied in trying to restore them in one way or another to their former glory. A few will search for total authenticity, but the majority will prefer to recreate a Victorian atmosphere by reintroducing original features without sacrificing twentieth–century standards of convenience. The aim of this book, therefore, is to provide them with details of the main constituents of Victorian house style, both inside and out, so that they can achieve this.

First, however, it is important to describe how Victorian domestic architecture developed during the nineteenth century. Unlike previous centuries when one architectural form predominated at a time, the nineteenth century became known for its 'battle of styles'.

For the first thirty years of the century, and to a lesser extent up until the 1850s, the classical style of the Georgian and Regency periods continued to be fashionable, with its stately, symmetrical forms, stucco façades, dignified Greek columns, pediments, balustrades and cornices, and simple decorative motifs. Inspiration also came from Italy and Italianate houses, resembling Renaissance villas, began to be built, with shallow – pitched roofs, overhanging eaves and rounded Romanesque arches framing windows and doors, embellished with scrolled brackets, pilasters and pediments. This was a style adopted by Queen Victoria for her new residence on the Isle of Wight, Osborne House, constructed between 1845 and 1851, which also included a tall campanile. Italianate features soon began to appear on the exteriors of many middle–class villas and terraced houses and continued to be popular right up until the 1860s.

However, by the mid–1850s a new style appeared which embraced the Christian architecture of medieval times. This Gothic Revival movement was first influenced by Augustus Welby Pugin (1812–52) and his design for the new Houses of Parliament, whose first phase – the House of Lords – had been opened in 1847. Pugin believed that Renaissance art forms with their symbols of heathen mythology had resulted in a revival of paganism and he therefore called for a return to the spiritually uplifting qualities of ecclesiastical architecture. This new moral tone was echoed by John Ruskin (1819–1900), who thought that houses should be sacred edifices. Overawed by the beauty of the carved stonework in Venice, Ruskin stressed in his book, *The Stones of Venice* (1851–3), the purity of individual craftsmanship and condemned the spiritual sterility of mass production.

The best example of Victorian Gothic architecture is Pugin's Scarisbrick Hall in Lancashire, which was remodelled into a medieval manor house. Built of stone, its features include a battlemented pitched roof with a central pinnacle lantern, a great hall, and extensive richly carved decoration. Soon countless suburban villas were adopting Gothic features, from steeply pitched roofs with turrets and towers, to pointed arches around doors and windows, all of which combined an ecclesiastical look with picturesque ornamentation. This style particularly appealed to the middle classes as it provided their homes with extra decorative forms with which to proclaim their growing prosperity while, at the same time, reflecting the period's renewed religious zeal.

Another great influence on Victorian style at this time was the Great Exhibition of 1851, held at the newly built Crystal Palace. Its aim was to show the world the diversity and excellence of British design and manufacture – as well as exhibiting the products of other nations – and was visited by vast numbers of people. Heralded as the arbiter of good taste, its displays of excessively decorated, mass–produced furnishings and furniture soon found their way into numerous middle–class homes. However, it was against this over–ornate, High Victorian style that the leaders of the Arts and Crafts movement later rebelled.

During the 1850s and 1860s, other styles also appeared which were influenced by the feelings of patriotism and nationalism stirred up by Sir Walter Scott's Waverley novels. Queen Victoria's house in Aberdeen-shire, Balmoral, adopted a Scottish Baronial style, whose features included battlemented parapets, crow–stepped gables, the introduction of a main tower and an overall castellated character. Elizabethan forms of architecture were revived as well. These styles, however, were normally to be found on large country houses.

By the 1870s, Ruskin's romantic ideals had been expanded on by William Morris (1834–96), father–figure of the Arts and Crafts movement which today has become most synonymous with Victorian style. With his belief that

Far left top: Classical forms and floral designs were the predominant decorative motifs during the nineteenth century.
Far left below: With the mass production of wall tiles from the 1870s, flowered picture tiles such as these soon adorned the porch entrances of even simple terraced houses.

Left: Many Victorian terraced houses had eye–catching black–and–white tiles in a variety of geometric patterns on the paths leading to their front doors. Below: In 1894 one design manual was giving advice on how to convert the no–longer fashionable rosewood chiffonier into a small drawing–room bookcase.

good art and design could only be achieved by hand craftsmanship, and that there should be nothing in the home which was not useful or thought to be beautiful, Morris revolutionised the decorative arts with his designs for wall hangings, fabrics, stained glass, carpets, furniture and metalwork. The house built for him by Philip Webb in 1859, The Red House, summed up his thoughts on architecture: built of red brick, with asymmetrical windows, steeply pitched roof with gables and a turret, carved wood interior and exposed brick fireplaces, it reflected 'vernacular architecture' – the art of the local builder using traditional techniques, local materials and individually crafted interiors.

The Red House became the prototype of the Queen Anne Revival style, the leading exponent of which was Richard Norman Shaw (1831–1912). Inspired by Morris, Shaw developed a style which created a feeling of 'sweetness and light'. Its features included warm red brick with contrasting white stonework; large bay windows or long, narrow ones with small, leaded panes, which emphasised the importance of light; and steep, patterned, tiled roofs with tall chimneys and Dutch gables. These details were incorporated into his designs for the

These highly ornate pieces of furniture and ornaments epitomise the over–decorated High Victorian style on show at the Great Exhibition. In reaction, the leaders of the Arts and Crafts movement turned back to nature and to simple, traditional craftsmanship for their inspiration.

London suburb of Bedford Park, which was begun in 1875; it was soon widely copied and became the most popular form of housing until well into the twentieth century.

The Queen Anne Revival was the form of architecture associated with the Aesthetic movement, which took hold in the 1890s but whose ideas had originally been put forward by Charles Eastlake in his *Hints on Household Taste* published in 1878. Eastlake deplored the fact that mass production had led to the imposition of style on people and believed, instead, that homes should reflect the individuality of their owners. He also advocated the use of lighter, more 'aesthetic' styles, with simplicity being the desired effect. This was quickly adopted by the Aesthetes of the day, together with the fashion for all things Japanese – imported into the country for the first time by Arthur Lasenby Liberty and sold in his new store, Liberty of Regent Street.

The end of the nineteenth century saw the birth of the 'Free Style' phase of the Arts and Crafts movement, whose most famous protagonists were Charles F. Annesley Voysey (1857–1941), Charles Rennie Mackintosh (1868–1928) and Edwin L. Lutyens (1869–1944). Voysey's houses were designed to look as if they were part of their natural environment and resembled simple cottages, with low roofs, wide eaves, horizontal windows, white roughcast walls, and exposed beams and brickwork. Mackintosh, who has been heralded as a precursor of the Modern movement, believed that everything in a house, right down to the smallest detail, should be designed to complement each other. The best examples of his work are to be found in his native Scotland, although his influence was strongly felt on the Continent and in America. Lutyens, on the other hand, was initially fascinated by the architecture of his home county, Surrey, and built houses out of local stone which resembled country cottages; later, however, he became renowned for his more formal architectural designs for large, country houses and public buildings.

Art Nouveau, which flourished between 1892 and the early 1900s, developed in Paris and predominated mostly on the Continent. However, its sinuous, curving forms with floral motifs were adopted by English designers for some interior features, notably glassware and metalwork. A number of stores also imported the work of Art Nouveau artists and craftsmen, so that examples of this new style could be seen in many fashionable late–Victorian homes.

By the end of the Victorian era, simplicity of design, although not along the classical lines in vogue at the beginning of the century, had returned, thus completing the cycle of the many different styles battling for influence during Victoria's long reign. The reaction against highly ornamented exteriors and eclectic styles of interior decoration (described later), so fashionable for much of the nineteenth century, made way for the birth of the Modern movement and the simpler lines of the twentieth century.

Chapter 1
The Plan and Façade

'However small and compact the house may be, the family must have privacy and the servants commodiousness; and the whole dwelling must display an unassuming grace. If, on the other hand, the circumstances of the owner and his tastes are such that magnitude and refinement ought to expand into state, even grandeur must not be pretentious, or wealth ostentatious, and the attributes of an agreeable English home must never be sacrificed....They form, taken as a whole, the test of a Gentleman's House: Privacy, Comfort, Convenience, Spaciousness, Compactness, Light and Air, Salubrity, Aspect and Prospect, Cheerfulness, Elegance, Importance, Ornament.'

Robert Kerr, *The Gentleman's House* (1864)

Opposite: With the rapid growth of the suburbs, streets of terraced houses such as this soon sprang up throughout the country. **Below:** Single–storey bay windows and porches framed by simple columns with moulded capitals were typical features of many early Victorian terraces.

Domestic housing in Queen Victoria's England underwent a radical change during her long reign as a result of the massive increase in demand for homes for the new monied middle classes. However, although banded together as one 'class', the range in incomes and professions – and therefore in the scale of their housing requirements – varied enormously. From rich, self–made industrialists to lowly clerks, the overwhelming desire they had in common was to have a house and a garden of their own, even if this meant going to one of the further suburbs – a possibility now that commuting had become cheaper. They emulated the various architectural styles adopted by the aristocracy, albeit in less expensive forms, and some of the better–off families even owned a country house, which they hoped would be their entrée into Society. The number of domestic servants in a household was also a status symbol, with virtually one in five families having at least one. As a result, the pattern of life in a Victorian household would have been surprisingly similar, but with varying degrees of simplicity, between the upper and the lower–middle classes.

On the whole, Victorian housing fell into four categories, depending on one's social status. The

aristocracy and the very wealthy had their large estates, with imposing mansions set in acres of land, plus an elegant house in town; next came the smaller detached house built in the new, tree–lined suburbs with a moderate sized garden; then there would be the semi–detached villa, one of the more common forms of Victorian homes, which would have a small front garden with a slightly larger one at the back; and finally the terraced house with its small back garden (although later terraces had a tiny area in front as well) However, those living in semi–detached villas or terraces, which together formed the majority of nineteenth–century housing, ranged from the aristocracy in their stately Belgravia homes to the lower classes in their more humble dwellings.

Except for in the homes of the poor, the hallmark of a Victorian house was space and privacy, with each room having its own particular place in the life of the household. Activities in the house were kept separate, with rooms used exclusively for the family, for entertaining, for visiting guests and for servants. As F. Hooper wrote in 1887, 'The various departments of the household must be distinct, with ready communications by doorways placed wisely to increase privacy...', while Robert Kerr in *The Gentleman's House* insisted that, 'however small the establishment, the Servants' Department shall be separated from the Main House, so that what passes on either side of the boundary shall be both invisible and inaudible on the other'. In his view, this was to be achieved by a system of numerous passageways and corridors throughout the house.

Examples of different styles of detached Victorian villas. **Opposite:** top, A Cottage Lodge in the Old English Style', c.1835; **middle,** an American clapboard seaside cottage, c.1880; **bottom left,** the side elevation of an Elizabethan style house; **bottom right,** a Queen Anne Revival house designed by Richard Norman Shaw in 1878. **This page, top,** architect William Burges's medieval style house in Kensington, c.1870; **middle,** a 'middle–class cottage' designed by Norman Shaw in 1878; **bottom,** a Scottish Baronial cottage', c.1860. **Below:** A house in Yorkshire designed by G. Dean in the Old English style, c.1860; **bottom:** The Red House, designed by Philip Webb for William Morris in 1859.

Large country houses or detached villas belonging to the wealthy usually had, on the ground floor, an entrance hall, a drawing room, a dining room, a living room, a morning room, a breakfast room, a smoking room, a billiards room and a library, all of which comprised the area inhabited by the family and their guests. The servants' quarters – the kitchen, the scullery, the pantry, the bakery, the laundry and the servants' hall – were also found on the ground floor. The first floor, approached by a grand staircase for the family and guests and a small back staircase for the servants, housed the bedrooms, with the men's being well segregated from the women's. Servants' rooms and children's nurseries were usually in the attic.

As we have noted, one of the predominant forms of town dwelling was the terraced house, which varied from the substantial classically proportioned home of the wealthy to the small two–up, two–down belonging to the poorer occupant. Many of the aristocracy, who considered their country home as their main residence, were happy to live in a terraced house in town, albeit one of the more spacious ones, even though it was inhabited by servants for large parts of the year.

Like their Georgian predecessors, these houses had basements in which the kitchens and service rooms were situated. These included the butler's pantry, the housekeeper's room, the store room, the pantry, the scullery, the laundry, the servants' hall and rear vaults for storing coal. The kitchen, at the front of the house, looked on to the 'area', a small open space enclosed by railings and reached by a steep flight of steps, which served as a separate tradesmen's entrance. On the ground floor was the entrance hall, the dining room and the library, with a grand staircase sweeping up to the drawing rooms on the first floor. The bedrooms were on the upper storeys, with the servants' rooms and children's nursery situated in the attic. To the rear of the house would be a mews in which the horses and carriages were stabled.

Opposite far left: Towards the end of the nineteenth century, the middle classes wanted their bays to extend up to the first floor so that the front bedroom could benefit from the additional space.
Top: Holly Village in north London, a Gothic Revival estate built in 1865 by Baroness Burdett–Coutts for her retired servants. The architect was Henry Astley Darbishire. **Bottom:** Simple carved gables and decorative red brickwork enliven an otherwise plain grey–stone façade.

Top: Four–storey terraced houses were inhabited by wealthier Victorian families as more floors were added to accommodate their needs. Note the different styles of windows, which provide a uniform row with an interesting design feature. **Left:** An American Victorian clapboard house, painted in a traditional pale colour scheme. **Above:** A row of Queen Anne Revival houses, incorporating all the elements of this architectural style: Dutch gables, tall chimneys, bay windows and warm red bricks decorated with white stonework.

Despite the number of rooms in a terraced house, the basic plan until the 1870s was the same: a front–to–back arrangement with each floor being two rooms deep and one room wide. The variation was in the height of the building, with extra storeys accommodating the additional rooms needed to serve the family's social position and size. Therefore, a large twenty–room mansion would conform to this overall plan but over six floors, whilst a more modest house would have a basement and two storeys, with further rooms up in the roof.

However, from the mid–1870s basements virtually disappeared as a result of the Public Health Act of 1875 and the growing awareness of the hygiene problems caused by damp areas below ground. From then on, therefore, the average house was entered on the ground floor and had three storeys, with the kitchen, washrooms and indoor or outdoor water closet housed in a back extension. The entrance hall, front parlour and dining room were also on the ground floor. The main bedroom would be in the large, front room on the first floor, with another one behind, and further bedrooms on the second floor. By the end of Queen Victoria's reign, these houses only had two storeys, with extra bedrooms and a bathroom on the first floor of the back extension; in some houses these extensions disappeared altogether, their rooms incorporated into the main body of the house.

For ordinary families, one of the gauges of their social position was whether they had a front parlour in which to receive guests and a separate dining room. These distinguished them from poorer households where the kitchen, heated by a fire and the cooking range, served as the room where the family lived, ate and washed, although by the end of the century some of these also had a parlour for 'best'. However, these smaller houses rarely had an entrance hall and the front door opened straight into the parlour.

Only in the heavy industrial areas did back–to–back terraced houses appear. In order to keep land and building costs low and to cover the ground with as many houses as possible, which usually resulted in a decline in building standards, these double rows of terraces, built with a party wall at the back as well as at the sides (which, incidentally, provided better insulation), became a common form of architecture for poorer housing in the new factory towns.

From the late 1880s until well into the beginning of the twentieth century, however, the pattern of house building began to alter. Terraced housing still continued to be popular, with its traditional front–to–back plan, but the development of vernacular architecture, as displayed on the new Queen Anne and Arts and Crafts style of houses, led to a squarer plan being adopted, with rooms leading off a large, central hallway. These houses were either detached or semi–detached, were situated in the new leafy suburbs built along the lines of Norman Shaw's Bedford Park development, and were usually of two storeys with no basement but with an attic. Even a modest home

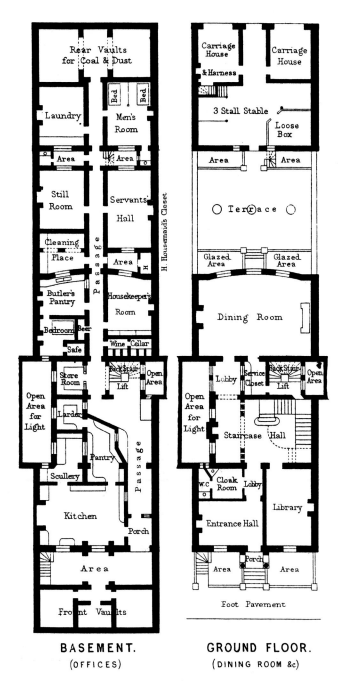

BASEMENT.
(OFFICES)

GROUND FLOOR.
(DINING ROOM &c)

The perfect layout for a row of
London houses, as advocated
by Robert Kerr in his book,
The Gentleman's House, 1864.

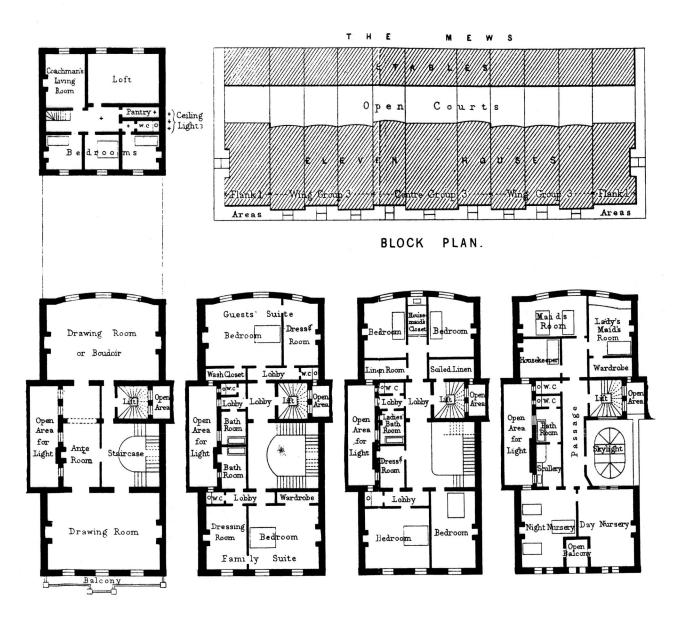

BLOCK PLAN.

FIRST FLOOR.
(DRAWING ROOMS)

SECOND FLOOR.
(CHIEF BEDROOMS)

THIRD FLOOR.
(SECONDARY BEDROOMS)

FOURTH FLOOR.
(NURSERIES &
SERVANTS' ROOMS)

would now have a morning room, as well as a living and a dining room, and an internal toilet and bathroom, which by 1880 were included in most new houses.

In contrast to Continental families, the Victorians were house dwellers, with flats being unpopular in England throughout the nineteenth century; even by 1911 only three per cent of the population lived in them. The middle classes did not want to inhabit flats as they thought of them as housing for the poor, a reference to the sheltered homes provided by charitable employers for their workers. However, most of these estates were not blocks of purpose–built flats as we know them today, but 'cottage flats' or 'half houses' – typical, two–storeyed terraced houses but with a flat on each floor and with their own front entrance. It was only towards the end of the century that local authorities began to clear inner–city slums and rehouse people in blocks of flats. However, a few impressive–looking blocks were built in the last third of the century which catered for the wealthier occupant, but flat dwelling did not really catch on until the twentieth century.

Left: One of London's elegant stucco-fronted streets, with glazed porches supported by decorative ironwork. **Below left:** A row of Gothic villas, c.1880. **Below:** The upper storeys of the house, where the servants' and children's quarters were, had smaller windows and little external decoration. **Bottom left:** A late Georgian terrace, a style still popular until the 1850s. **Bottom Right:** A simple canopy on decorative brackets forms a shelter from the weather for visitors to this early Victorian terraced house.

Opposite top: From the 1870s Americans rejected neutral colour schemes and painted their clapboard houses in bold, imaginative tones. **Left:** An elegant row of brick terraced houses embellished with white stonework decoration and ornate railings bordering the front steps. **Right:** Even a modest terraced house was given an imposing entrance porch with carved stonework and columns inspired by Ruskin's *The Stones of Venice*.

Creating an impression was of great importance in the Victorian era and the exterior of the house was as much an indicator of the occupier's wealth and status as the interior. Complimenting the different architectural styles of the period (described in the Introduction), the façades of Victorian houses were embellished with a variety of decorative details, with practical features being as ornamented as those added for purely aesthetic reasons. With widespread use of such details as patterned tiling and brickwork, elegant ironwork on railings and balconies, elaborate gables, Gothic spires, and columned or arched porches, porticoes, door and window surrounds, even a simple house acquired some degree of external ornamentation. One of the pleasures of looking at Victorian houses in whatever price bracket is the variety of details adorning their façades.

Roofs and Gables

The most common type of roof found on Victorian houses is the sloping, pitched one, which in England was usually covered with tiles or grey Welsh slate; in America, however, wood was used more frequently.

At the end of the Georgian and the beginning of the Victorian eras, the roofs of houses tended to be hidden from street view behind parapet walls, which gave an appearance of elegant uniformity to a row of terraced houses. Whilst it looked as though there ought to be a flat roof behind the parapet, there was actually a shallow-pitched roof, placed at right angles to it. Where the two adjoining roof slopes met in a central valley, a lead-lined gutter would run along it. The problem with this was that rainwater accumulated in the centre of each house and could cause extensive damage.

By the middle of the century, roofs had become visible and thus targets for decoration. Villas and semi-detached houses in the Italianate style still had shallow-pitched roofs, but the overhanging eaves where the roof projected over the wall were now supported by brackets which were moulded or carved in the shape of scrolls and flowers, acanthus leaves being particularly common. On neo-Gothic houses, roofs acquired an ecclesiastical look with dramatic, steeply-pitched sides, often topped with pointed spires, turrets and towers. Queen Anne Revival roofs, however, were hipped (pyramid-shaped), with every kind of decoration on them from tall chimneys, roof tiles of different hues forming complex patterns, Dutch gables and finials in the shape of miniature spires, crosses or globes. Mansard roofs, which had a flat top and near vertical sloping sides, became popular in France during the 1860s and were later to be found on some British and American buildings; their steep sides were effective places to display complex tiled patterns.

Gables, the triangular upper part of a wall between the sloping ends of a pitched roof, formed another feature ripe for decoration and were often trimmed with elaborate plasterwork and mouldings. These gables, repeated above doorways and over the tops of bay

As soon as roofs became visible in the middle of the nineteenth century, every part of them was ripe for embellishment, from decorative ridge tiles and ironwork finials (opposite) to carved gables and multi–shaped chimneys. The façade below is decorated with overlapping fish–scale tiles and a balcony inset into its gable.

Top far right: A cornice of different–coloured tiles adds decoration to an ordinary roof, as do the patterned ridge tiles. **Top right:** With the Gothic Revival movement, chimneys became more prominent. This one complements the grey slate tiles, the most popular form of Victorian roofing material. **Middle and below right:** Fretwork gables and contrasting–coloured brick quoins and lintels provide attractive decorative features. **Below:** Roofs decorated with diamond patterns became popular in the 1870s. **Opposite top:** A 'gingerbread' house in Suffolk built in 1860. **Opposite far right:** A picturesque row of chess–piece chimney pots enhances the overall decoration of this house. **Opposite right:** Ecclesiastical influences were strongly felt on many Gothic Revival houses.

windows, became a common feature on many Victorian suburban houses. Intricate patterns of contrasting coloured tiles were also to be found on the gables of many Queen Anne Revival buildings, with overlapping fish–scale tiles and diamond designs being popular, whilst Victorian 'gingerbread' houses had richly carved and painted wooden trims at the peak of their gables. Wood was also used on the prominent, half–timbered gables of some late–Victorian 'Tudor' style houses.

Roof crests became fashionable on buildings from the 1880s, either of tiles or of iron. Decorative tiles in a different shape and colour from the main roofing material would be laid along the ridge of the roof, ending in a small, upright finial often in the shape of an acanthus leaf or a honeysuckle branch; or ornamental ironwork, topped with spearheads, fleurs–de–lys and other symbols, was used to form a miniature railing along the ridge of the roof. Chimneys were also to be found in a variety of elaborate styles, including in the shape of chess pieces.

Gutters were originally made of wood or lead, but by the middle of the nineteenth century zinc and iron were most commonly used. Drainpipes were also made of iron and provided yet another source of decoration, with rainwater heads often having the date of the building or some other emblem on them.

A variety of wall tiles illustrating some of the floral motifs popular in the Victorian era.

Decorative Brickwork and Tiles

Until the cost of transportation was drastically reduced with the improvement in railways and roads, most houses were built with local materials such as stone and granite. Bricks were manufactured as near as possible to the site where they were to be used, with most small towns having a nearby brickworks, but by the middle of the century they became more widely available due to better production techniques, the repeal of the brick tax in 1850 and cheaper distribution around the country. As a result, brick began to be used more frequently not only for construction but also for decorative purposes. The colour and constituent elements of the bricks varied according to where they were made – for example, London had a yellow variety – but red became the dominant colour adopted by the vernacular architects from the 1870s until the end of the century.

Decorative brickwork adorned most Victorian houses in some form or other, especially during the mid–Victorian era when it became fashionable for façades to be embellished with a variety of different colours and surfaces. As a result, contrasting coloured bricks were used as arches over porches and doorways; as lintels; as ornamental cornices and friezes under the eaves; and inset into walls and roofs in a profusion of different patterns, including geometric, diamond and trefoil shapes.

In the first half of the nineteenth century stucco was the most popular material used on the façades of houses. A hard plaster with a smooth finish which could then be painted, it was originally made of a mixture of lime mortar and sand, although later cement mortar replaced the lime. Not only did it provide the normally thin external walls with a protective waterproof coat, but it also gave an elegant appearance to a building. Many city streets were transformed by the stately, stucco–fronted terraces built during the early years of Victoria's reign. Some of these were completely covered with stucco, whilst others only had it on the ground floor, and it was often grooved to look like blocks of stone. It could also be easily moulded into numerous forms and soon stucco–covered balustrades, cornices, pediments, architraves, quoins and porches with columns and highly decorated capitals sporting floral or classical motifs adorned many a building. Even simple houses acquired a dignified exterior with the use of stucco around windows and doors, embellished with arches, pediments and columns. However, by the 1860s stucco fell out of favour, although vernacular architects later used it in the form of pargeting a mixture of cement and rough sand, which could be carved into more intricate designs.

Except where local stone was easily quarried and therefore cheaper than brick, stone was more often used as decoration on the facades of buildings than in their construction. This was especially true from the 1860s, when the improved cost of quarrying and transportation coincided with the Gothic Revival movement and its rediscovery of the beauty of carved stonework. From the

Sculptured terracotta and stone panels, quoins and finials were a particular feature of Queen Anne Revival houses.

Top right: Late Victorian porch entrances were often inset with decorative tiled wall panels.
Top and right: In the second half of the nineteenth century encaustic–tiled pavements in lozenge patterns and geometric shapes appeared on the front paths of many suburban houses. As well as being durable, their warm, natural clay colours were also welcoming. **Above:** Patterned terracotta was used for decorative cornices and lintels from the 1860s.

1880s, it was also used for lintels, balustrades and as ornamentation around bay windows.

Terracotta became a popular substitute for brick and stone from the 1860s. At first it was only available in red and yellow, but gradually a wider range of colours – including pink, grey and tawny – began to be produced. Because it had an impervious finish, it was used to face entire buildings in polluted industrial areas, although it was more popular as a decorative feature. On Queen Anne style houses, sculptured terracotta panels displaying geometric or floral motifs – the sunflower was the most common – were inset into external walls, under the eaves, or between doors and windows. It also faced balustrades, quoins, door and window surrounds, and even porches, and terracotta tiles in the shape of fish scales, or laid in geometric or herringbone patterns, decorated roofs, gables and walls.

Tiles were not used on the façades of buildings although William Morris thought that homes should be covered with them, both for aesthetic reasons and for easy maintenance. However, his view was not adopted and the Victorians tended to use tiles just to decorate the pathways to their front doors, and the floors and walls of their porches. Hard–wearing tasselated tiles made of dense, baked clay became popular for paths, laid in geometrical black and white designs, diagonal stripes and lozenge patterns. In natural colours of dull red, brown, ochre and black – as well as other artificial hues – they provided a pleasing entrance to the house. Wall tiles with sun, flower, herb and bird designs ornamented the inside of the porch, often with a tiled picture of a pastoral scene inset in them.

Top: A good example of how different patterned brickwork was used by Victorian architects to enliven the exterior of a house. **Left:** Panels of patterned tiles were also to be found on external walls.

Porches, Verandahs and Balconies

Porches, which provided an impressive–looking entrance as well as giving shelter from the weather, were a popular feature of Victorian houses. They originally extended beyond the house and covered the bridge above the 'area', but after basements began to disappear from the mid–1870s, they began to be incorporated into the main building as a recess by the front door.

Porches with column supports built out from the external walls would originally have been of stone, but in the early Victorian era painted stucco became the material most popularly used. Applied over brickwork or wood, the stucco could be moulded into complicated styles, and rows of elegant stucco–fronted houses with classical–columned porches graced many of London's streets right up until the 1870s. These were also ornamented with architraves, cornices and a frieze, surmounted by a balustrade.

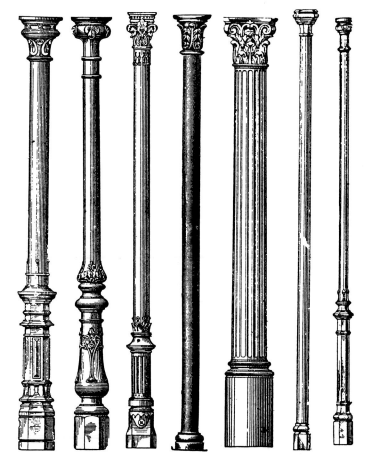

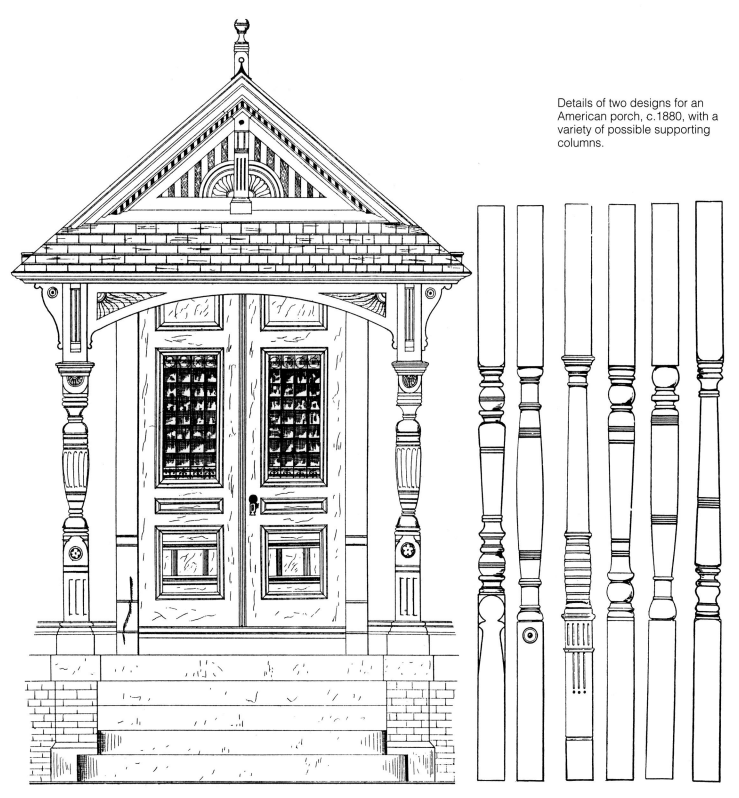

Details of two designs for an American porch, c.1880, with a variety of possible supporting columns.

A variety of porch designs were in evidence throughout the nineteenth century, including stucco porticoes flanked by round Greek or square Italianate columns; Gothic porches framed by carved, pointed arches; simple trellises made of wood or iron; glazed canopies edged and supported by decorative ironwork (made possible with the invention of larger panes of glass and the abolition of the glass tax); and terracotta–faced porches and canopies, sometimes shell–shaped at the top, which became popular in the 1870s.

Simple recessed openings or larger recessed porches aligned with the bay of the windows became a common feature of late Victorian suburban houses and provided ordinary homes with a dignified entrance, which could then be further enhanced by decorative floor and wall tiles.

Verandahs – or 'porches' as the Americans called them – were viewed as an outside living room, where families relaxed on wickerwork furniture during the good weather. Cool to sit on, they also served to keep the temperature of the house down by protecting the outside walls from the sun. In America and Australia, with their long, hot summer days, the verandah was an essential addition to the house and fine examples in highly decorated wood or iron are to be found on many Victorian houses. However, they were less common in England, although they are to be found in some grander homes and country villas.

English porches ranged from stately structures with classical forms to simple bracketed canopies.

With low pitched or flat roofs (so that the main building was not obscured) supported by graceful columns, which reflected the style of the house, they also featured ornamental railings, elaborate roof brackets with a variety of motifs, and decorated balusters and balustrades which adopted the same design as the brackets. As one contemporary catalogue advertised, its ornamental verandah included 'friezes, moulded gutter and cresting for front and returns', columns with entablatures, brackets, frieze, gutter and pediments, with glazed roof and ironwork frame.

Verandahs were sometimes added to the façade of a building on the first floor, often with an iron roof and elaborately detailed ironwork supports and railings.

Opposite: Victorian designs for ornamental verandahs and balconies. **Below:** A classical porch would have simple balustrades, cornices, friezes and architraves supported by either (from left to right) Tuscan, Doric, Colonial, Ionic or Corinthian columns.

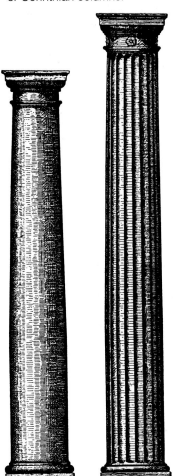
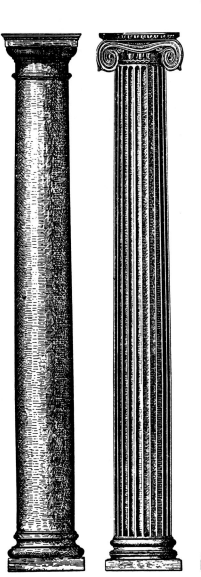

Balconies were another feature on the outside of houses, although used primarily for decoration. They were more common in the early Victorian era, however, because of the popular pastime of looking at what was going on in the street. Once mass–produced iron became available from the 1820s, graceful ironwork balconies became a regular addition to the outside of houses. This was especially true in Australia and America, where the famous lacework found in Melbourne and the spectacular ironwork of the American South show how intricately detailed the designs could be.

First–floor balconies sculptured around the bay or bow of a window normally had a wrought–iron frame with cast–iron decoration, the anthemia – a heart and honeysuckle – becoming the most fashionable motif. More modest suburban houses did not have elaborate ironwork balconies but were frequently built with a simple balcony projecting below a window with a stone floor and painted stone or wooden railings.

Decorative iron window guards and grilles also appeared as additional ornamentation.

Opposite and left: With improvements in mass production, intricately worked cast–iron porches, balconies and railings became widely available during the Victorian era. **Below left:** In the first half of the nineteenth century, it was fashionable to view what was happening outside from graceful ironwork balconies such as this. **Below:** A Victorian Gothic porch.

Ornamental cast–iron gates and railings announced to the outside world the status of the family within; thus the more elaborately decorated they were, the better. The sinuous forms of some Art Nouveau designs were particularly suited to wrought ironwork – for example, the bottom gates on the opposite page.

Railings and Gates

As the property–owning class grew during the Victorian era, so did the practice of marking the borders of one's territory with railings and gates. These became more decorative from the 1820s with the increase in the variety of ironwork styles being mass produced. With the publication of pattern books by Coalbrookdale, Carron and other firms, the Victorian house–owner was greeted with a wealth of designs from which to choose, although these were less delicate than their eighteenth–century counterparts due to the greater use of cast iron, which was less malleable than wrought iron.

On a terraced house, the 'area' was enclosed by simple railings, with ornamental tips in a number of shapes including spearheads, fleurs–de–lys, crosses, pineapples and pine cones. The gate leading to the front door, which was often taller than today's garden gate, was more elaborately decorated. Front gardens and houses without an 'area' were also fenced in with cast–iron railings and a gate, although wood and wrought iron were used later in the century by the Arts and Crafts movement.

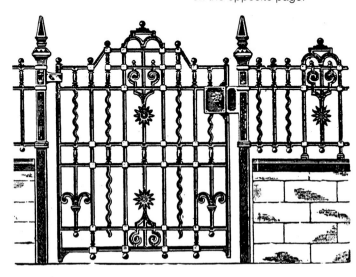

To delineate the boundaries of their property, Victorians could choose from a wide variety of railings, from simple sticks with a decorative top to more ornate patterns.

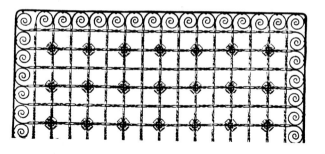

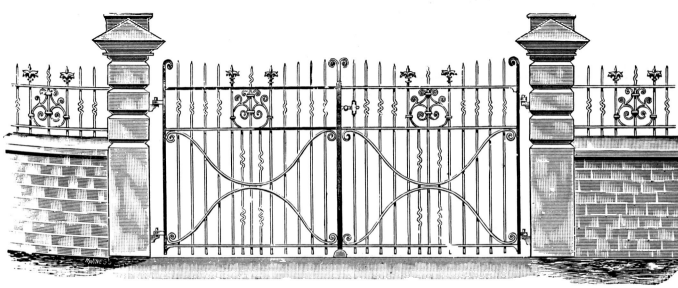

Some late–Victorian designs for gates, railings and bell-pulls.

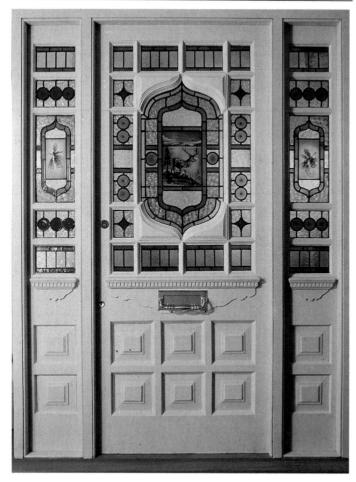

Doors

To the Victorians, the front door of the house made an important statement about the wealth and position of its occupants and therefore had to convey the appropriate impression to anyone approaching its entrance. The solid, wood–panelled door of the eighteenth century with its semi–circular fanlight above – the only way of allowing light into the hallway – was replaced in the nineteenth century by a variety of designs echoing the diversity of architectural styles. Each front door, therefore, mirrored the individual style of the house itself.

Doors were nearly always panelled and elaborately carved. To enhance their stature, they would be surrounded by a door frame with an imposing architrave, carved and panelled to match the door and then painted or grained to look like a more expensive wood, for example oak. These door frames ranged from Classical pillars to Gothic pointed arches of coloured brick or carved stone, or elegant woodwork panels inset with stained glass. With gleaming brass door furniture, polished daily by the household's domestic servants, the overall effect, even on a small house, would have been impressive.

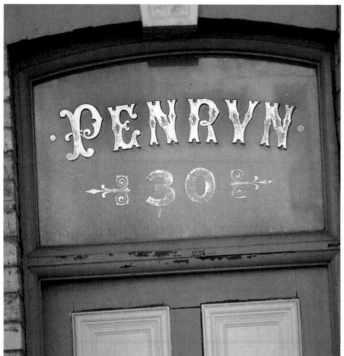

Opposite top: Front doors inset with stained–glass panels depicting scenes from nature became very fashionable in the 1880s, inspired by William Morris's designs for this revived craft. *London Door Company* **Opposite below left:** The name and number of this house etched into the fanlight provide an ordinary front door with some decoration; right: an Italianate front door, c.1860, is framed by classical marble columns. **This page:** Whatever the style or status of the house, an imposing front door inset with glass panels was an essential feature of most Victorian entrances.

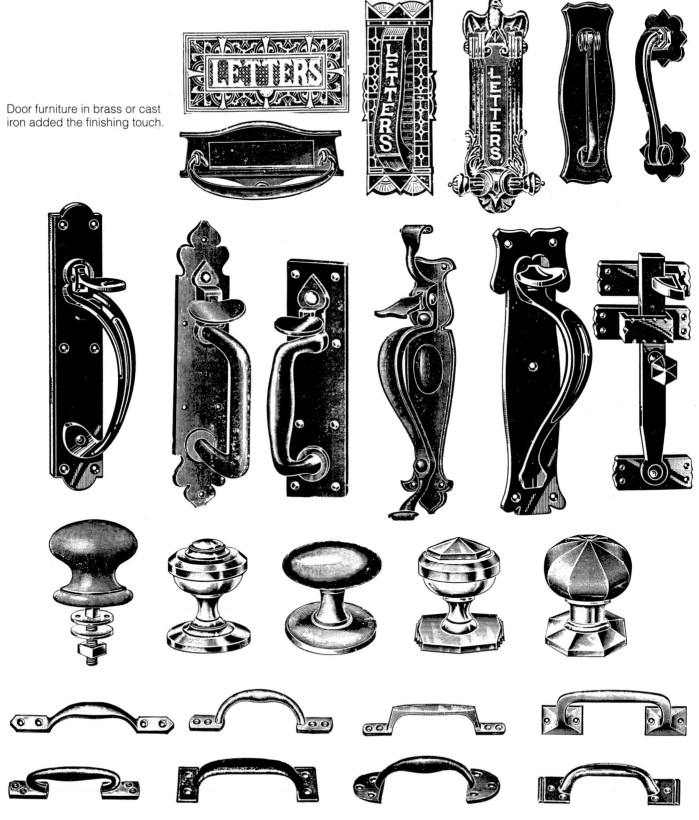

Door furniture in brass or cast iron added the finishing touch.

Where there was no porch, some doors had a hood above them – a moulded, projecting lintel which was supposed to protect one from the rain. These were usually painted and sometimes elaborately carved, so that even a simple front door could look interesting.

With the growth of the suburbs and of terraced housing, the front door had to conform with the others in the street so as to preserve the uniformity of design. One door painted another colour to the rest or replaced by a competing style could bring disharmony to the whole street, whereas co-ordinated differences – for example, a row of doors painted in complimentary colours on purpose – could create an attractive pattern. Colours used became brighter during the century and doors were often painted with a two-tone effect.

The position of doors also varied on terraced houses, with the door/window, door/window pattern being replaced by one of window/door, door/window. When 'cottage flats' began to be built, the entrance often had two identical front doors next to each other, one for each flat.

Many doors still had fanlights above them, either traditional Georgian semi-circular ones decorated with intricate ironwork designs of spiderwebs, circles and loops, or simpler square ones. However the development of glazing and the manufacture of larger panes of glass in the late 1830s enabled glass to be incorporated into the front door itself. Initially only the two upper panels were glazed, but by the 1880s the entire top half of a door might include several leaded panes, inset with patterned, coloured glass.

The Gothic Revival and the Arts and Crafts movement in the middle of the century resulted in a resurgence of interest in the use of stained glass. Doors were soon being decorated with beautiful glass panels, created by William Morris, with floral patterns and designs based on medieval themes. As well as forming a pattern by setting coloured pieces of glass in lead, Morris also encouraged the art of painting on the glass itself. Towards the end of the century, when Art Nouveau became fashionable, its sinuous forms and curved shapes were well suited to the art of stained glass.

In contrast to the impressive front door of the upper- and middle-class house, many simple homes had a basic wooden ledged door – made of tongue and groove boarding nailed to three horizontal planks of wood, or ledges; these were then strengthened by diagonal planks between the ledges. The ledged door was also to be found on back entrances as well.

Door Furniture

Cast iron was the popular material used on door furniture in the first half of the century, with designs for door knobs, knockers, locks and hinges echoing the themes of the previous century – for example, shields, lions' heads, medusas, dolphins, urns and lyres. By 1850 the use of brass became more widespread and front doors with shining brass bell–pulls, finger–plates and letter boxes were an inviting sight. Cast–iron foot scrapers were also a traditional feature beside a front door, although they are no longer in use today. Street numbers engraved on glass panels or in metal also began to appear on front doors.

When restoring or replacing the front door of a Victorian house, care must be taken to find one that echoes the character of the house and those in the rest of the street. Salvage yards are good sources for original doors, which provide authenticity, especially if they have retained their carvings or stained–glass panels. An alternative is to copy the original door, which will have the added advantage of fitting perfectly and giving better protection from draughts. Skilled craftsmen can restore stained glass or reproduce panels to replace damaged ones, whilst many Victorian patterns are still being manufactured today. Individual designs can also be specially commissioned to bring a more modern look to a Victorian house. Original door furniture can also be easily found, although modern reproductions are widely available.

Above: An ornate early Victorian door knocker, with a ram's head, embellishes a solid wood–panelled door.
Right: The style of this graceful Georgian fanlight, with its Coade stone voussoirs, was copied on early Victorian buildings. Later, stucco was used instead of stone.

Left: Gleaming brass door furniture found its way on to many front doors from the 1850s, especially now that even the middle classes had servants to polish it. **Below left:** This front entrance, set into the bay of the house, combines many of the popular design features of the late–Victorian period.
Below: From the 1870s etched glass was also inset into door panels.

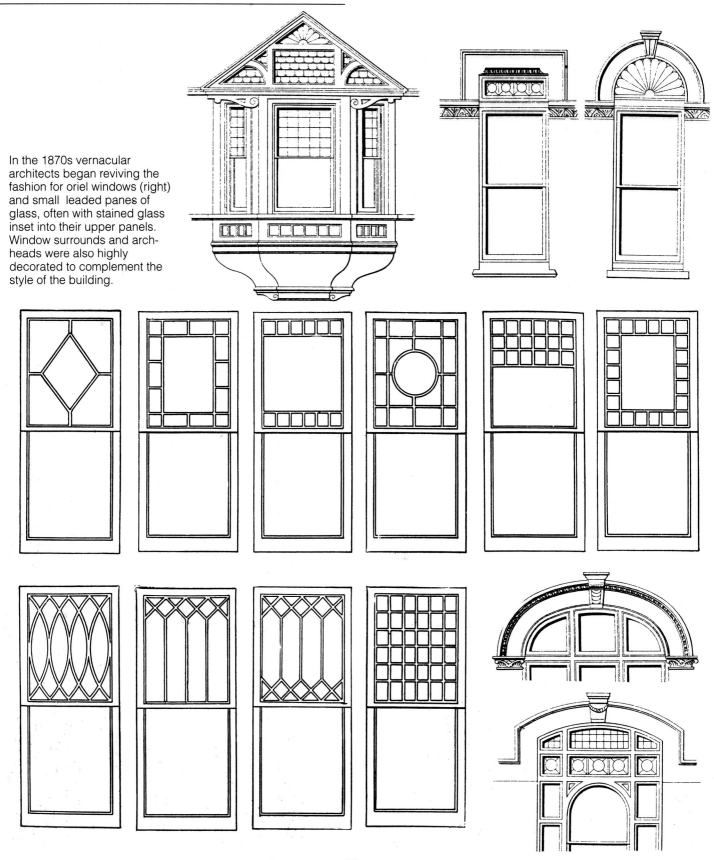

In the 1870s vernacular architects began reviving the fashion for oriel windows (right) and small leaded panes of glass, often with stained glass inset into their upper panels. Window surrounds and arch-heads were also highly decorated to complement the style of the building.

Windows

At the start of Victoria's reign, the common form of window was the twelve–paned, vertical–sliding sash found in most Georgian and Regency houses. But with the abolition of window tax in 1851 and of the duty on glass in 1857, along with the commercial availability of polished sheet glass after 1838, this was soon replaced by six– and then four–paned windows. As T. Webster wrote in 1844 in *An Encyclopedia of Domestic Economy:* 'The abundant introduction of light, by means of large panes of glass, adds a cheerfulness formerly unknown.'

As a result, Victorian architects began to revive the use of bay and bow windows, which allowed in more light, gave more space and a feeling of elegance to a room, and provided a distinctive feature to an otherwise simple façade. Bay windows had originally been popular in the late eighteenth century in country houses and seaside villas, which gave the occupants a better view of what was going on outside. Rounded bow windows were adopted for some classical town houses in 1840, and by the mid–1860s large square or polygonal bays, with the sash window incorporated into the bay, had become the rule for the ground floor of most suburban houses. By the end of the century, even the standard working–class parlour had a bay window, but by then the middle classes were demanding that the bay be carried up to the next storey to include the front bedroom.

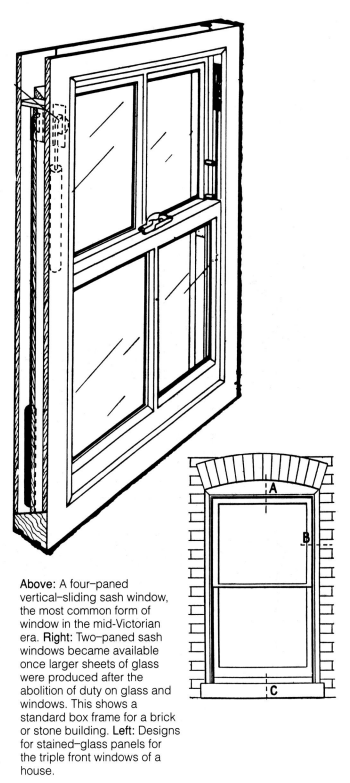

Above: A four–paned vertical–sliding sash window, the most common form of window in the mid-Victorian era. **Right:** Two–paned sash windows became available once larger sheets of glass were produced after the abolition of duty on glass and windows. This shows a standard box frame for a brick or stone building. **Left:** Designs for stained–glass panels for the triple front windows of a house.

Ironically, it was just as larger panes of glass became more affordable that the Gothic Revival movement reintroduced small casement windows – hinged vertically to the window frame – and leaded lights. Some later Victorian houses incorporated both styles, with the lower floors having large–paned windows and the upper storeys having small, leaded panes instead.

Oriel windows were also used on upper levels for lighting bedrooms and staircases. These were small bays cantilevered off the main structure of the building and supported underneath by timber or metal brackets, which provided an additional decorative feature. This was a popular type of window, although it rarely appeared on terraced houses. The Arts and Crafts movement used them – the Red House designed for William Morris by Philip Webb had several oriel windows – as did architect Norman Shaw on his Queen Anne Revival houses.

Above: A traditional late–Victorian suburban house with two-storey bay windows framed with simple white stone architraves and columns. Its elegance is enhanced by the contrasting–coloured brickwork cornice under the eaves and between the storeys. **Top right:** Although some Gothic houses had lancet (pointed arch) windows, many had plain sash windows with carved stonework surrounds. **Right:** A late–Victorian terraced house with a square bay and Queen Anne–style sash windows.

Left: Lancet–shaped glass panes were often inset into a square–framed sash window to provide a Gothic feature in the mid– to late–nineteenth century. **Below:** An early Victorian twelve–paned sash window.

Around the window was vast scope for decoration. Bays often had a hipped gable placed artificially above a cornice; lintels and window caps were ornamented with carvings; Gothic windows had pointed, medieval arches of stone or brick; and many modest homes had their windows framed by multi-coloured brickwork patterns and such adornments as Romanesque arches supported by capitals of carved foliage – a Venetian style inspired by Ruskin.

Unlike Europe and America, British windows did not normally have external wooden or ironwork shutters. These almost always appeared on the inside of the window.

As with door panels, stained-glass windows enjoyed great popularity in the nineteenth century. From 1820, large panes of glass surrounded by a narrow border with blue or red corners with a star cut into them were commonly used in French windows and staircase landings. However, the wave of romantic nostalgia which prevailed in the middle of the century and the resurgance of interest in the art of stained glass led to the floral motifs and medieval themes of William Morris becoming widely adopted as window decoration. Later, stained-glass design was dominated by the stongly curved patterns of the Art Nouveau movement. However, as mass-produced copies replaced individually hand-crafted windows, and the market became flooded, a backlash soon ensued: by the beginning of the twentieth century and the start of the Edwardian era, 'pure' glass, not decorated, became the vogue.

From the 1850s many English and American firms began mass producing a wide range of patterns for bevelled and leaded plain–glass windows. These are some of the designs to be found in their catalogues c.1890.

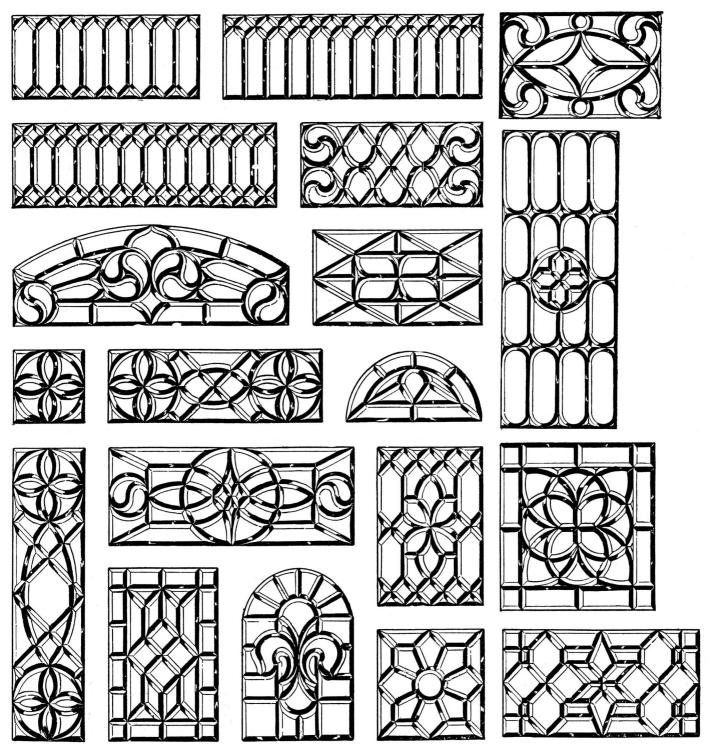

Right: A round–arched Italianate–style window with a decorative ironwork window guard. Below: The warm brown colours and floral theme are typical of the stained–glass windows designed by the Arts and Crafts movement from the 1870s. Below right: Some late Victorian homes adopted the use of external shutters.

In America, the master of stained–glass design, Louis Comfort Tiffany, created magnificent pictorial windows – richly coloured landscapes and plant studies as well as heroic and biblical themes. Though originally commissioned for churches and public buildings, his influence was soon found in the home as commercial glaziers began to produce stained–glass pictures better suited to domestic decor – for example, country scenes. Thus, many Americans were able to install scenic windows into their houses ordered from the manufacturers' pattern books.

Despite the return to clear windows at the end of the Victorian era, the widespread use of stained glass on front doors and windows during the nineteenth century provided many homes with a delightful decorative feature, whose legacy we are still enjoying today. Not only did the light shining through the coloured glass create a glowing effect inside, but the stained glass also preserved privacy while at the same time providing an attractive picture for the passer–by to look at.

Left: This Gothic window has its original, vertical–sliding shutters. **Below left:** Simple lancet windows, Gothic arched window hoods and wooden decoration give this house a medieval look. **Below:** Many Victorian houses had square sash windows on one storey with rounded Italianate ones on another.

A variety of different patterns both for plain- and stained-glass windows manufactured by Victorian firms in the late-nineteenth century.

Chapter 2
Hallways, Stairs, Landings and Bedrooms

'The Entrance–Hall is an apartment of so many characteristic varieties that it may almost be taken as a criterion of the class to which the house belongs. In a case of the least ambitious order it will be no more than a wide passage from the Entrance–Hall to the staircase ... whereas in a first–class Mansion it will be a spacious and perhaps stately apartment... decorated with paintings and statuary, ancestral armour and the trophie of the chase.'

Robert Kerr, *The Gentleman's House* (1864)

Opposite: The hall at 18 Stafford Terrace, the home of *Punch* cartoonist Linley Sambourne. The carpet was designed by John Henry Dearle for Morris & Co. c.1890.
Below: Vestibules were not only another form of decoration but also provided practical insulation.
Plain–glass panes were often inset into the vestibule door so that the rich colours and patterns of the stained–glass front door could be seen in the hallway.

Once through the front door, the hallway was the next place where the family's social position could be gauged as this was where visitors were received. Powerful first impressions could be formed, especially if a glimpse was caught, through an open door, of the grandest rooms of the house – the drawing room or the parlour. The hall was also a thoroughfare from the cold and dirt of the outside world to the warmth and security of the home.

Although grand houses had large, imposing entrance halls, most Victorian terraced houses had a long, narrow hallway, with doors leading off to the reception rooms. As the hall was designed to impress, it would be richly decorated with elaborate panelling, high ceilings adorned with ornamental plasterwork, and patterned floor tiles. There would be little room for furniture, but whatever pieces there were would usually be of oak or mahogany. There would normally be a wooden stand to hold coats, hats and umbrellas, flanked by a couple of chairs for waiting visitors. From the middle of the century, these stands were also available in cast iron and were often over–elaborately designed. One trade catalogue of the period was advertising 'Intricate iron casting, bronzed and marbled, arranged with pedestals for hats, coats and umbrellas, containing also a pillar for a lamp and looking glass with boxes both for letters, brushes and an inkstand.' However, if the stand was a simpler one, without a shelf or drawer to hold visitors' calling cards, there would normally be a separate, narrow

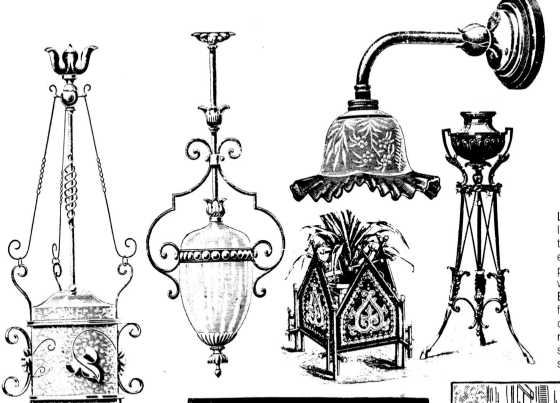

Left: Hanging oil or gas lanterns and wall brackets lit the usually dim Victorian entrance hall, whilst potted plants in ornate *jardinières* were placed everywhere.
Bottom left: 'Mural Decoration for a Dado', Charles Eastlake's design for a hall, 1878; middle: one of William Morris's stained-glass panels; right: the staircase at The Red House.

table as well. An oak or mahogany grandfather clock completed the scene.

Whilst an important feature of a large hall was an inviting fireplace, some narrow hallways also managed to find room for one. Apart from being an extra decorative item, a fire provided heat on entering the house and combated any draughts from the front door and the staircase.

Despite the fact that most hallways were dark, with very little natural light coming in through the fanlight or through the front door's stained–glass panels, the entrance hall was invariably decorated in strong, dark colours which gave an impression of richness and warmth. This was supplemented by the dim, but welcoming, light from hanging oil and gas lanterns.

Below left: Delicate hall chairs or benches, c.1830s, gave way to over–ornate furniture from the 1850s, such as this cast–iron umbrella stand, with its bird decoration (bottom middle). **Below right:** A selection of designs for wooden stair balusters. **Bottom left and right:** Open fires and later radiators were a feature of many entrance halls, even narrow ones, as they provided warmth on entering the house.

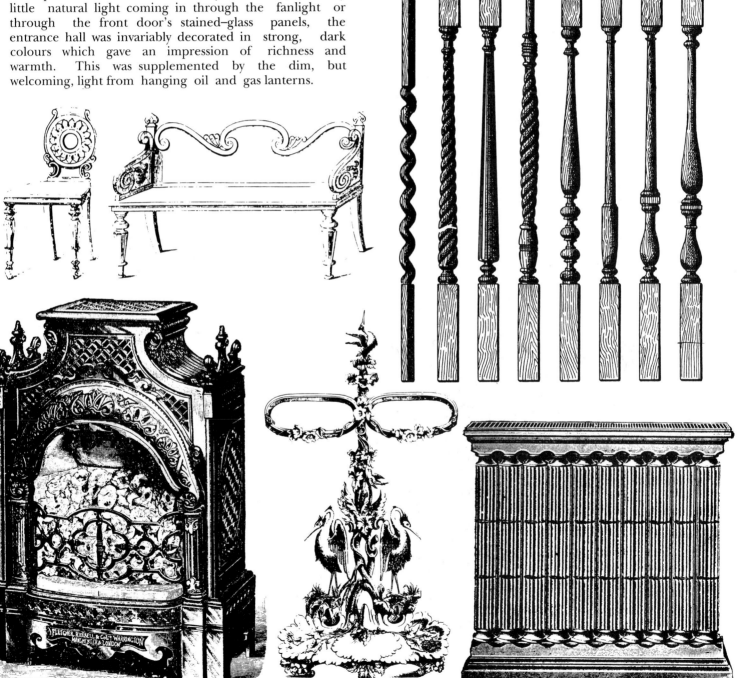

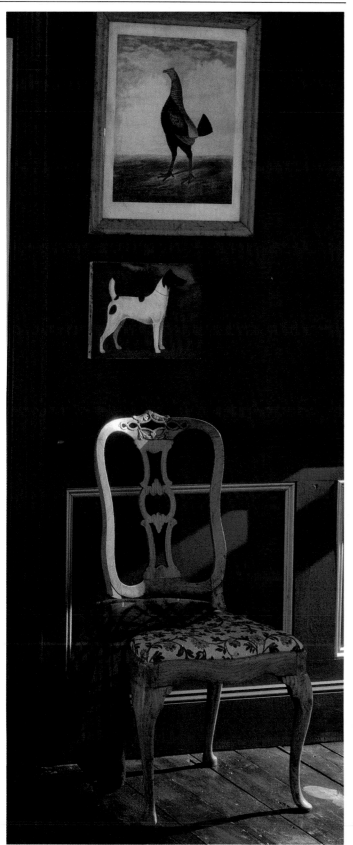

The lower half of the walls either had wainscoting – panels of mahogany or oak, or a soft wood grained to look like them – or a dado covered with embossed papers like anaglypta or Lincrusta, which were then varnished or painted with special effects to simulate leather or individual slabs of marble. Around the 1870s, however, encaustic tiles began to be used on dados and provided a hard-wearing and washable wall covering of about three or four feet in height. Above the dado, the walls were decorated with heavily patterned wallpapers, with deep shades of green and burgundy predominating.

The walls would then be hung with paintings – narrow hallways having small pictures framed in maple wood, with 'no subject requiring thought and study [being] suitable in such a position' (Edith Wharton), and larger ones having a gallery of imposing family portraits. A mirror might also be placed above the fireplace or the hall table.

Opposite: Dados with panels or decorated in a contrasting colour to the rest of the wall were a traditional feature of most Victorian hallways and landings from the 1870s. These two have been decorated in the popular colours of the time: Prussian blue, sage green and burgundy. **Left:** An authentic-looking late-Victorian hallway, with its geometrically patterned encaustic tiles, stained-glass front door and mahogany hall stand. **Above:** A simple staircase lit by a stained-glass lantern.

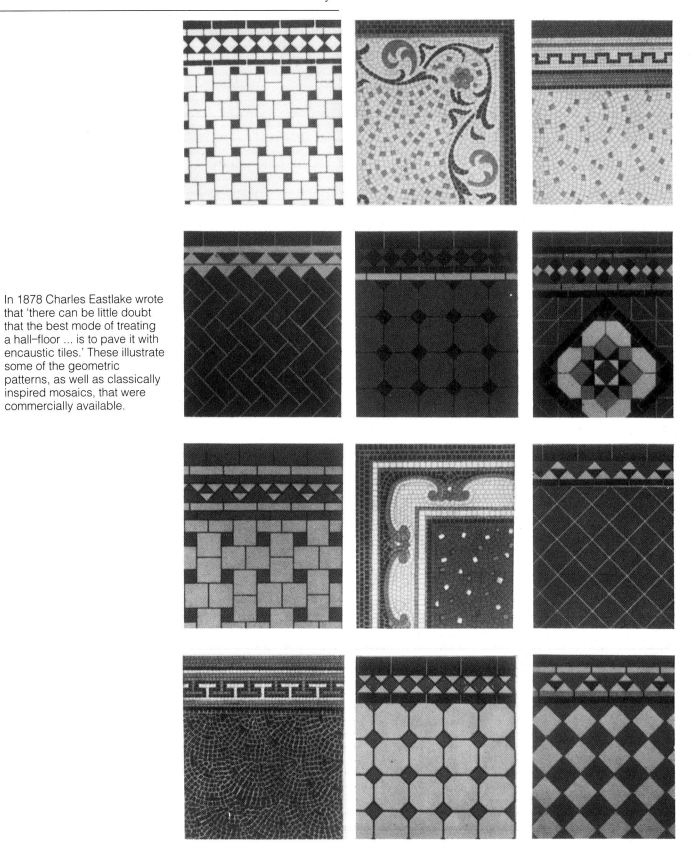

In 1878 Charles Eastlake wrote that 'there can be little doubt that the best mode of treating a hall–floor ... is to pave it with encaustic tiles.' These illustrate some of the geometric patterns, as well as classically inspired mosaics, that were commercially available.

With all the dirt coming into the house from the outside, floors had to have surfaces that were hard-wearing and easy to clean. Up until the 1850s, the most popular flooring was oilcloth – either plain or patterned – or wooden parquet covered with small rugs, but these were superseded by encaustic tiles, which began to be commercially manufactured around the 1840s. Laid in 'medieval' or geometric patterns of different coloured clays, these soon became highly fashionable. Later in the century, mosaic floors of black and white marble and coloured stone were also to be found.

The long, narrow hallway of the Victorian terraced house was broken up in a number of ways. A regular device was the addition of a vestibule, a small porch between the entrance door and the main hall partitioned off by a glass-panelled door. With its fine carving and beautiful beveled, frosted or stained-glass, this door protected the house from draughts and added another elegant feature to the hallway. These doorways would sometimes be draped with heavy curtains, hung on wooden or brass poles and looped back for easy access. Other devices were the addition of decorative arches or ornamental fretwork across the hallway.

With the Gothic Revival movement came the idea that the hall was a central feature of the house. In larger homes, imitations of medieval Great Halls began to appear, rising up two storeys and often with a first-floor gallery with doors leading off to the bedrooms. These halls were decorated with dark wood-panelled walls, beamed ceilings, inglenook fireplaces, large latticed windows with the top panes of glass patterned with coats of arms and other heraldic symbols, and stone or mosaic-patterned floors covered with Oriental rugs. The walls would be hung with tapestries and paintings, and the room filled with suits of armour; statuary of marble, bronze or terracotta; and majolica plant stands, terracotta *jardiniéres* and elegant wire baskets full of exotic foliage and flowers.

Pugin, who revived the medieval style of architecture, described his design for the hall at Alton Towers in Staffordshire in a letter to the Earl of Shrewsbury: 'As regards the hall I have nailed my colours to the mast – a bay window, high open roof, two good fireplaces, a great sideboard, screen, minstrell gallery – all or none , whilst a visitor to William Morris's Red House was surprised to find that 'the hall appeared to one accustomed to the narrow ugliness of the usual middle-class dwelling of those days as being grand and severely simple. A solid oak table with trestle-like legs stood in the middle of the red-tiled floor, while a fireplace gave a hospitable look....'

By the 1870s, these Great Halls had begun to be used as additional living rooms, with lower ceilings and plainer decor, and by the 1880s even modest homes were being built with larger entrance halls. These had wider front doors with latticed windows on either side, and conformed to the squarer plan adopted by the vernacular architects.

Staircases and Landings

Whilst large Victorian houses had grand staircases and simple houses, with the front door opening on to the front room, had a cased–in staircase with a modest flight of steps leading from a corner of the back room, the middle–class terraced house and semi–detached villa had an important–looking staircase at the end of the entrance hall with a broader bottom step curving round at the ends to give an additional flourish. Staircases became simpler on the upper floors, and where there was a basement a plain, boxed–in staircase led down to the kitchen and servants' quarters.

The stairs were often built of stone and carpeted with a central runner held in place with gleaming brass carpet rods. On wooden staircases, the treads outside the carpet area were painted, usually in a rich shade of brown.

The newel post was still a prominent feature of the staircase, although in the nineteenth century it was viewed merely as a functional end to the handrail. Less elaborate than its eighteenth–century counterpart, it varied from being of solid, carved wood to being a simple cluster of wooden sticks.

Handrails were of smooth hardwood, often of mahogany, with ornamental cast–iron or carved wood balustrades. These were either fully panelled, half–panelled or with balusters resting on the stairs themselves – usually three per step in a large house, and two per step in a smaller one. The balusters were often of quite complex designs, scrolled and twisted into floral and Gothic shapes or carved into intricate fretwork, although simple, stick balusters became more fashionable towards the end of the century.

However, staircases became more ornate when the Arts and Craft movement reintroduced the grand staircase into the home and when the sinuous Art Nouveau motifs, translated into curved metal and woodwork, became popular.

The first–floor landing was usually large, with landings becoming smaller on the upper storeys. This was especially true in houses where the drawing room was on the first floor. Here an impressive landing was required on which to receive guests and from where the hostess could lead them into the principal reception room. This landing would be lit by a sash window, often with stained–glass panels in it.

According to Robert Kerr, in his *The Gentleman's House* (1864), landing windows should preferably face north so that there would be no glare from the sun; as a result, blinds would become unnecessary. He also disliked the idea of ceiling lights on a staircase, except where walls were covered by pictures which needed appropriate lighting, and felt that the landing window should provide all the light and ventilation required. However, when back extensions became a common feature of houses from the 1870s, the landing was often lit by a small skylight as it was now an internal area without access to an outside wall.

Opposite left: These encaustic–tiled pavements and borders produced by Maw & Co. of Salop were considered by Eastlake to be 'unrivalled'; **right:** Australia's ornamental cast–ironwork became world–famous from the 1880s. At Medley Hall near Melbourne, this intricately worked staircase leads down to a stunning encaustic–tiled hall floor. **This page:** Even ordinary staircases were decorated with carved balusters and newel posts.

Bedrooms

Up until the beginning of the nineteenth century, bedrooms were also used as living rooms, but the growing desire for privacy meant that for most Victorian families the bedroom soon became a separate room. The main bedrooms were sited on the first floor above the reception rooms while the children and servants had rooms on ascending floors. The nursery was often in the attic.

In many Victorian households, the husband and wife would have their own bedroom, with a connecting door in-between, and a dressing room. Women often had a private boudoir or sitting room as well. Here they would rest during the day on a low couch, write letters at a small table, or read or do needlework sitting in a comfortable chair. Children of both sexes shared a nursery, but later moved into separate sex bedrooms as a result of nineteenth-century reformers insisting that older boys and girls be segregated. This meant that even the most humble home had to have an extra bedroom. Dressing rooms and back extensions were therefore converted to provide the additional space.

As concern for hygiene increased throughout the century, it was felt essential that bedrooms were kept simple, light and easy to clean. Not only were portable baths and chamber pots kept in them until bathrooms became more widely installed after the mid-1870s, but bedrooms were also used for giving birth in and as sick-rooms. Furniture, fabrics and decor, therefore, had to be polished, washed and redecorated frequently so as to avoid germs. Mrs Beeton in her *Book of Household Management* recommended opening bedroom windows for at least half an hour every morning to let in the air, although this allowed in the dust at the same time. As air changes in the room were thought necessary for a good night's sleep, fireplaces in every bedroom were advocated not only to provide warmth but also to encourage through drafts. Spring-cleaning, to remove all the dirt and dust that had accumulated over the winter from the smoke of oil or gas lamps and from burning coal or wood fires, was also carried out in every household.

Fireplaces became smaller and less ornate in the upper storeys of the house, and sometimes the attic rooms had none at all. They were normally made of wood or cast

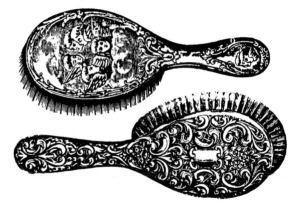

A selection of furniture and accessories that would have been found in a Victorian bedroom, including Eastlake's 1878 design for an iron bedstead with a half–tester canopy (opposite).

iron, with a simple register grate and surround, often painted white.

As the Victorian bedroom was a private room, which only members of the family and servants visited, it was kept simple with few architectural features in it. The essence of the room was comfort, with each lady of the house imprinting her own personality on it by adding a wealth of small, decorative details – often hand–made – which combined to give a unique, overall effect. Thus each bedroom reflected its owner's individuality and afforded 'a clue to the designer's and owner's special tastes and fancies' *(The Household)*. As a result, the Victorian bedroom is the easiest room in the house to recreate accurately because, with its simple shell, original decorative details can easily be added; fabrics and wallpaper patterns are still available; and the furniture and small items that provide the finishing touches can be found without difficulty either in antique shops or as modern reproductions.

Whilst the decor of the bedroom in some very grand houses echoed the opulence of the reception rooms, in the average home the bedroom was kept bright and feminine, often adopting a neo–rococo or Louis Seize style. Walls were painted in white or pale colours – pinks, sea greens, grey or blues – and were washed down or repainted regularly. From the late 1870s, when thinner, lighter wallpapers were manufactured, printed patterns of flowers, fruit and ribbons became popular alternatives. Nursery papers also appeared at this time with patterns based on characters and scenes from children's books.

The only architectural detail in the bedroom would be a cornice, which was simpler than those in the rest of the house and which would often be painted in a contrasting colour, picking out a colour from the fabrics in the room. A frieze or a hand–stencilled border were other decorative devices used.

Floors were left uncarpeted so that they could be scrubbed frequently. Sanded wooden boards were covered with rush matting, Oriental or rag rugs, which could easily be taken up and cleaned. In the nursery, linoleum was also used, as it was hard–wearing and washable, covered with bright hearth rugs with fairy–tale scenes on them.

Bedroom Furniture

With the importance of the family in Victorian life and the increased number of children conceived, the main feature in the room was the bed. In *The Gentleman's House* (1864), Robert Kerr speaks of the bedhead being placed 'to the wall after the English manner', as opposed to the French custom of putting the bed in an alcove with one side to the wall, so that the room looked more like a parlour.

When Queen Victoria came to the throne in 1837, beds were four–postered, made out of mahogany or beechwood, and curtained off completely for privacy and warmth. As concern grew that the heavy drapes harboured dust and germs, wooden or iron half–testers, with

Opposite top: Victorian bedrooms were feminine in character and filled with hand–made decorative objects, like this lace bedspread and scattered cushions. The stained–glass windows also give the room a period feel, although a Victorian bathroom would not have been en–suite with the bedroom. **Opposite bottom:** By the 1860s, simple brass beds such as this became fashionable as they were considered to be more hygienic than heavily draped half–testers.

Left: It is easy to recreate a Victorian bedroom just by the use of lavish drapes around the bed. **Above:** There would often be several small tables covered with hand–made tablecloths, candles, mirrors, flowers and other *objets* in a Victorian bedroom.

Washstands, shaving stands, towel rails and dressing tables were essential items of bedroom furniture. However, whilst the mid–Victorians indulged their love of over–decoration and fussy fabric treatments, even on dressing–tables, the Arts and Crafts movement preferred their furniture to be ornamented with simple carving, patterned tiles and detailed metalwork.

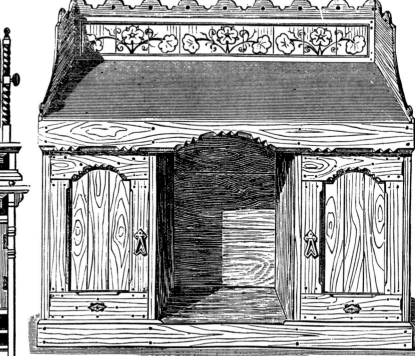

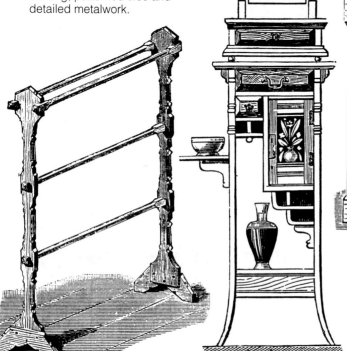

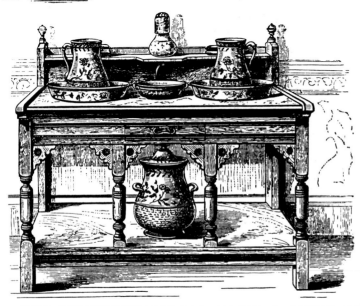

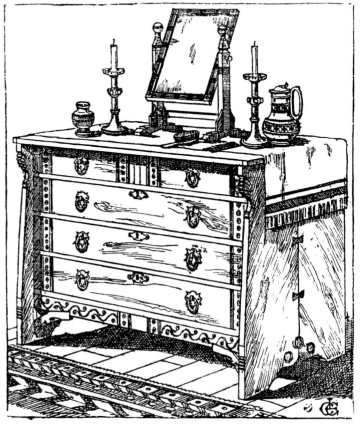

decorative canopies extending about three and a half feet over the headboard, became fashionable. Elizabeth Burton in *The Early Victorians at Home* describes them thus: 'This ungainly kind of bed often had two tall, square posts at its head which rose seven or eight feet above floor level. About three–quarters of the way up, huge projecting scrolls were attached.' From the posts were hung chintz or cretonne curtains, which during the day 'were looped back and held in place by heavily tasselled cords'. Headboards and footboards were elaborately carved in a variety of styles, and ornamental brass beds with a half–tester construction also became popular: 'The whole bedstead was a riotous mélange of styles; the half–tester, a hangover from late medieval times; strap–work, Elizabethan; curves, scrolls and curlicues, heavy–handed baroque; paterae, eighteenth–century neo–classical; bellflower, decorated Gothic.'

However, for hygienic reasons, by the 1860s many people preferred to sleep in simple brass beds with no hangings and by the 1880s it was recommended that those half–testers still in use only project about one and a half feet.

The drapes around the bed and the window curtains were normally of the same fabric, with one of the colours in it being picked out on the cornice; it was also fashionable to use the same material for tablecloths, pillows and dressing–table covers. Delicate floral chintzes, lace, cretonnes, white dimity, and dotted, striped or sprigged muslins were popular, trimmed with lengths of antique lace, ribbon or fringing. These would be festooned, pleated, ruffled, swagged or draped and would be hung on wooden rods. Only in wealthy houses were heavy fabrics, such as velvet, silk or brocade, used. Behind the curtains there would also be a light muslin blind, wooden Venetian blinds or wooden shutters.

The next largest piece of furniture in the room was the wardrobe, with the 'winged' variety – a double wardrobe with a central mirrored section – being the most prestigious style to have. These large cupboards, often over six feet tall, were a far cry from the simple hooks on which clothes were hung at the beginning of the century. However, a cheaper, simpler alternative was a brass curtain rail across a chimney recess with a pretty chintz curtain in front, as suggested by *Cassell's Household Guide*. By the 1890s, the architects of the Arts and Crafts movement were advocating built–in furniture and fitted cupboards in the bedroom began to be popular.

Dressing–tables were another important feature in the room and were usually placed in the bay of the window. They were normally draped in muslin edged with ribbon or lace, with a calico underskirt, and 'Duchesse' dressing–tables also had a toilet mirror attached to them. The tops would be covered with silver–capped perfume bottles; ivory or silver combs and brushes; candlesticks; *papier–mâché*, mother of pearl, silver or beadwork boxes; and numerous other trinkets.

Robert Kerr wrote that bedrooms should also be furnished with a small writing table, 'a pier–glass with its back to the light', a low couch and easy chairs, and a chest of drawers. This furniture was usually an odd assortment of pieces that were no longer considered fashionable or good enough to be on public display in the reception rooms. Although there was often quite a lot of furniture in the room, a feeling of clutter was avoided because of its size.

In the middle of the century bedrooms achieved a more unified appearance because of the manufacture of matching suites of furniture, which included bedstands, wardrobes, mirrors, bureaus and washstands. These were made out of ornately carved and gilded wood – rosewood, mahogany or black walnut – although lighter woods were later used, including bamboo and fake bamboo, which reflected the vogue for Oriental *objets*.

As already mentioned, washing took place in the bedroom until the mid–1870s. With domestic servants available to carry water up and down the stairs, portable tubs and hip baths were brought in and placed in front of the fire. Wooden washstands, normally of mahogany, were permanently in the room, tucked away in a recess or alcove or hidden behind a screen. Early Victorian ones were three–cornered with a bow front and a cavity to hold the porcelain basin, whilst later washstands had a marble or wooden top with a tiled splashback, and a lower shelf. Water jugs, soap dishes and wash bowls, decorated with flowers or Oriental designs, were not only practical items but provided a touch of colour in the room. In a shared bedroom, the man's mahogany shaving stand would be placed in another corner of the room. This normally stood on a tripod base with ball or claw feet, and had a swing mirror and a wash bowl sitting on it, often with a towel rail attached.

Decorative items also added to the general warmth of the room – hanging bookshelves; botanical prints and other pictures; Japanese screens; needlework footstools; delicate chairs, bedheads, small tables and boxes made from *papier–mâché,* which was lacquered black and either inlaid with mother of pearl or decorated with painted flowers and fruit; dressing–table accessories; beadwork–covered boxes; home–made patchwork or lace bedcovers; and lots of assorted crocheted lace or embroidered cushions scattered everywhere.

Below: One can achieve a Victorian–style bedroom by finding original decorative items and pieces of furniture in antique and junk shops. Also, many traditional designs for lights, brass beds and fabrics are also being widely reproduced today. *Adrian Sankey*

Left: A heavy, carved mahogany bed was the most important item of furniture in a mid–Victorian bedroom. **Below:** The bedroom was one of the few rooms in the house that had very little architectural detail, just a pretty moulded cornice and a ceiling rose. As in this bedroom, pastel colours tended to predominate.

A selection of decorated washstands and basins, which featured in the 1888 J. L. Mott Ironworks catalogue.

Chapter 3
Living Rooms

'In [the drawing room] ladies receive calls throughout the afternoon, and the family and their guests assemble before dinner. After dinner the ladies withdraw to it....It is also the reception room for evening parties....The character to be always aimed at in a drawing room is especial cheerfulness, refinement of elegance, and what is called lightness as opposed to massiveness. Decoration and furniture ought therefore to be comparatively delicate; in short, the rule in everything is this ... to be entirely ladylike.'

Robert Kerr, The Gentleman's House (1864)

In a large Victorian house, the reception rooms comprised the drawing room, the dining room, the morning room, the billiard room, the smoking room and the library, whilst a simple middle–class home would merely have a parlour and a dining room. But however many living rooms a home possessed, it was here that the family's respectability and social status were assessed by the outside world. These rooms were therefore located in the best position in the house, had larger proportions and higher ceilings, had more elaborate architectural details and fireplaces, were filled with the owner's best furniture and were decorated with the most sumptuous furnishings.

The main reception room used for entertaining and special occasions was the drawing room, with everyday family life taking place in the morning room or parlour. In a terraced house with an adjoining front and back parlour, the front room would be kept for visitors with the back room used by the family.

As the Victorian woman spent much of her day at home, with domestic pursuits and creative activities such as needlework taking up a great deal of her time, the drawing room and parlour took on a feminine character, with an atmosphere of comfort and cosiness. In contrast, the dining room, library and billiard room were seen as male domains and were thus decorated in a darker, more masculine style.

Opposite: An Aesthetic drawing room, c.1880, with its tripartite wall – dado, central filling and deep frieze, each of which would have been decorated in a different way – and its plate rails displaying Oriental china. **Below:** The light, feminine styles of the late–Regency period were still in evidence in early Victorian drawing rooms.

The Drawing Room and Parlour

From the 1830s, the two influences that predominated in the drawing room were neo–rococo and Louis Seize, graceful, feminine styles characterised by florid ornamentation, gilt carving, elaborately moulded *papier – mâché* (and later plaster) cornices and ceiling medallions, elegant white marble fireplaces, pale silk damask wallpapers, rounded furniture, and heavily draped curtains and upholstery. The fireplace was the focal point of the room with furniture placed in conversational groupings. As the century progressed, however, more and more furniture was added to the room to show off the owner's prosperity, giving the drawing room and the parlour the overcrowded and over–fussy look so associated with the Victorian era. This fashion for over–furnishing reached its heyday in the 1870s and 1880s, but by the end of the century a reaction had set in against it with the Arts and Crafts movement introducing a lighter, less cluttered, decorative style.

Early in the Victorian era drawing rooms were decorated in pale colours, with cream, lavender, pearl grey, light green, pink and blue predominating. Originally walls were covered with panels of watered silk, damask or cotton (which was less expensive), surrounded by gilt moulding. However, with improvements in the production of wallpapers and the introduction of chemical dyes in the 1850s, patterned wallpapers in richer colours replaced fabric as wall decoration. Designs included scrolls, birds, vines, traceries and William Morris fruit and flowers, in such colours as plum, sage green, rose, gold, ochre and Prussian blue, though by the 1890s white and cream were back in favour.

Carpets were heavily patterned, often with cabbage roses or acanthus leaves, in dark green, scarlet or pink and white. Instead of being fitted from wall to wall, a two–foot–wide margin was left around the perimeter of the room, which was then either covered with oilcloth or linen, painted, marbled or decorated with patterned parquetry. By the mid–1870s, however, when concern for hygiene increased, simple, stained and polished wooden floors became the norm, covered with Oriental rugs. This style continued to be fashionable until the end of the century, when lighter floorboards strewn with a variety of handwoven rugs became a feature of Arts and Crafts homes.

Drawing–room curtains also became fussier as the century progressed and a typical High Victorian window would often have as many as four layers of curtains. First would be the 'glass curtain', a muslin or net curtain hanging next to the glass and covering the lower half of the window. Next would be a lace undercurtain, with a heavily draped outer curtain of velvet, damask, silk or brocade, elaborately trimmed with tassels, fringing or ribbons. Finally there would be an ornamental valance, or lambrequin. In the summer months, the heavy drapes would be taken down and replaced with lighter muslin curtains. But by the last quarter of the nineteenth

William Morris's swirling floral designs appeared on late–Victorian walls, floors and fabrics and have become synonymous with Victorian style.

The lines adopted by the Arts and Crafts movement (left) contrast greatly with the fussy fringes and frills preferred by the High Victorians.

Above: A handsome chimney–piece , like this Belgian rouge marble fireplace, c.1880, was felt to be essential in a Victorian dining room. This one at Wardlaw, near Melbourne, is complemented by a magnificent cornice and ceiling frieze.**Right:** An unusual feature of this white marble and enamel chimney piece is this elaborate circular over–mantel mirror. **Above right and opposite top:** Seamless Axminster carpets were commercially manufactured to imitate Oriental rugs. **Opposite bottom:** A Gothic Revival living room with original Victorian Gothic furniture.

century, curtains had become plainer and hung straight from a simple wooden or brass pole.

The lavish drapery of the curtains was echoed elsewhere in the room: doors were covered with heavy curtains (*portières*); fringed, velvet pelmets framed mirrors, pictures and mantelpieces; and chairs were upholstered in vivid floral patterns, with lavish trimmings and festoons of material draped between their legs.

The graceful, classical lines of Regency furniture were soon replaced by coarser styles as furniture became mass produced. Comfortable chairs and sofas became possible with the introduction of deep buttoning and coil springs in the 1850s and the Victorian drawing room was soon filled with big, horsehair or velvet sofas and Chesterfields, and a variety of styles of heavily stuffed, chairs. These included the crapaud, a toad–like arm chair with deep padding; ottomans; the prie–dieu, an elaborately carved, high–backed mahogany chair with tapestry upholstery; and the 'sociable', a pair of mahogany or walnut chairs linked together with button upholstery and ornamental fretwork. Balloon–backed chairs, painted bentwood and cane chairs, *papier–mâché* chairs and needlework footstools were also crammed into the room.

The High Victorian drawing room was also filled to the brim with ornaments and furniture. Card, sewing and

occasional tables of every style, often draped to the ground with velvet, chenille or lace cloths, were laden with *objets*, as were the obligatory rosewood or burrwood what–nots and *étagères*. Every surface was covered with porcelain figures, plates, clocks, stuffed birds and wax flowers under glass domes, candlesticks and lamps, albums and silver picture frames, whilst mirrors, paintings, miniatures, folding screens, firescreens of embroidered petit–point, plinths with marble busts on top, plant stands, *jardinières*, and a walnut piano – the chief sign of respectability – jostled for space around the room. In fact, the more overcrowded the room, the better.

However, by the late 1880s the Arts and Crafts movement had reintroduced simplicity into the home, with plainer decoration and less furniture made by old–fashioned joinery techniques. Traditional woods, like oak, yew and elm, were popular and chests, sideboards and settles had little surface ornament except for cut–out motifs – hearts and spearheads were the most common – and exposed brass or pewter fittings. Chairs were more upright with rush seats or leather upholstery, and furnishings were devoid of frills in naturalist designs based on William Morris's patterns. Gleaming pewter, hand–beaten copper, silver and brass were used for mirrors, light fittings and vases, whilst all things Oriental, especially Japanese, became fashionable. Fireplaces had either cast–iron surrounds, with decorative tiles inset in the sides, or large wooden, brick or ceramic–tiled chimneypieces with open hearths and free–standing grates; inglenook fireplaces also reappeared in Queen Anne Revival drawing rooms, sometimes with built–in seats.

At the end of the Victorian era, colours were paler, with furniture and woodwork often painted white, and styles more delicate. The overall effect was lighter and more harmonious, with the simple elegance of the neo–classical and Regency drawing room being recreated, but in a modern form.

A selection of drawing–room furniture c.1875. Many of the styles were recommended by Eastlake in his *Hints on Household Taste*.

The Dining Room

The Victorian dining room was decorated in a dark, masculine style and, unlike the cluttered drawing room, contained only a few pieces of imposing mahogany furniture. As Jane Loudon wrote in *The Lady's Country Companion* in 1845, 'The dining room should be char-acterised by the massive appearance of its furniture and the richness of its hangings. The curtains may be of maroon–coloured cloth or moreen, trimmed with gold. The carpet should be Turkey or Axminster, and should not quite cover the room but leave a part to be rubbed bright or painted. You should have a large handsome chimney–piece and a large grate, so contrived with a plate at the bottom, as to contain wood as well as coal.'

As it was the fashion to keep dining–room chairs lined up along the wall, dados and wainscoting appeared in this room so as to protect the walls from damage from chair–backs. However, by 1864 Robert Kerr was noting that 'In very superior rooms it is sometimes the practice to place the chairs, or a portion of them, when not in use, not against the wall, but around the table.'

Walls were usually decorated with deep crimson flock paper, on which sombre family portraits in heavy gilt frames were hung, and floors were soon fully carpeted. Occasionally a drugget – a coarse–cloth floor covering – was laid on top of the carpet underneath the table in order to avoid it being stained.

Opposite above: Stained-glass windows with heraldic motifs were fashionable in Arts and Crafts reception rooms. **Right:** A typical Victorian dining room with the table laid for supper as seen by Mrs Beeton.
Left: In this Victorian cottage the hob/grate in the dining room provides an area to heat food and boil a kettle. **Above:** The Victorians decorated and adorned every surface with bric-à-brac and floral patterns in sombre colours.

Left, from top to bottom: Two
early Victorian sideboards
with delicate carved
decoration;a sideboard with
Gothic features; examples of a
Gothic oak, a mahogany and a
padded–damask dining–room
chair; and an ornate sideboard
c.1855 which contrasts greatly
with the one designed by
Eastlake in 1878 (below).

One of the main pieces of furniture was the sideboard, which was taller and more ornate than its eighteenth century counterpart. It was normally in one of four styles – Elizabethan, Greek, Gothic or French – and of richly carved wood, with shelves supported by brackets in the form of leaves or pilasters, a heavy framed mirror at the back, and large recessed cupboards underneath. For example, one 1850s' sideboard described by Charles Eastlake was 'bowed in front and "shaped" at the back; the cupboard doors were bent inwards; the draw fronts were bent outwards, the angles were rounded off: tasteless mouldings were glued on; the whole surface glistened with varnish'. On the sideboard the family displayed its best silver, glass and porcelain.

In the centre of the room was a large mahogany table, which could be either circular, square or rectangular. When guests were being entertained, it would be dressed with 'graceful stands of silver, glass and porcelain, which hold flowers, and leave to every guest a full command of the table'. Because Victorian meals consisted of innumerable courses, chairs needed to be comfortable and solid in order to support people's weight throughout the lengthy repast. The most common style was the balloon-backed chair, of mahogany, walnut or rosewood, which was upholstered in stamped leather or a closely woven tapestry.

The Arts and Crafts dining room was greatly influenced by the style of interior decoration adopted by William Morris in his own home. As one visitor to The Red House described, the dining room had a long oak table in it, with plain black, rush-seated chairs, and a wide dresser reaching to the ceiling, ornamented with painted decoration. The brick fireplace whose chimney breast went 'up to within a short distance of the ceiling, where it finishes off with a covered top,' had a movable settle near it, 'with high back, the panels of it filled with leather, gilt and coloured .... The walls were tinted with pale distemper and the ceiling ornamented by hand in yellow on white.'

Early Victorian dining-room tables were more elegant than the heavy mahogany ones favoured in the 1850s. However, from the late 1870s Eastlake and Arts and Crafts members began to look to Jacobean and other Old English designs for their tables.

Right: A Victorian parlour can be conjured up by the addition of a hunting trophy, potted plants on pedestals and a cast–iron fireplace with a simple overmantel.

Opposite: Victorian billiard rooms were masculine retreats and were usually decorated with wooden floors, real or simulated wood–panelled walls,and dominant fireplaces. The top fireplace and mantelpiece are made entirely of cast iron.

Libraries and Billiard Rooms

As these rooms were primarily reserved for the men of the house, their decor 'should present a great contrast to the light elegance of the drawing room' (J.C.Loudon, 1838). Walls were simulated to look like marble or stone, with dados filled with wood panelling or imitation leather paper, and ceilings were high with richly moulded cornices. Often designed in an Elizabethan or Gothic style, the rooms contained large marble fireplaces, had dark crimson, bottle green or brown velvet curtains, and comfortable sofas and chairs upholstered in leather or velvet. Antique armour and stag heads mounted on the walls completed the scene.

In middle–class homes, the library often doubled up with the dining room, with marble busts placed on top of free–standing bookcases. In larger homes, bookcases were usually built in, with classical pediments and pilasters or moulded Gothic arches. A central mahogany or rosewood library table, on pedestal legs, and a writing desk were the other main items of furniture in the room.

Most grand houses also contained a billiard room, which was situated on the ground floor, often with a smoking room nearby. These were viewed as 'rakish retreats' and were sometimes decorated in a Moorish or Turkish style.

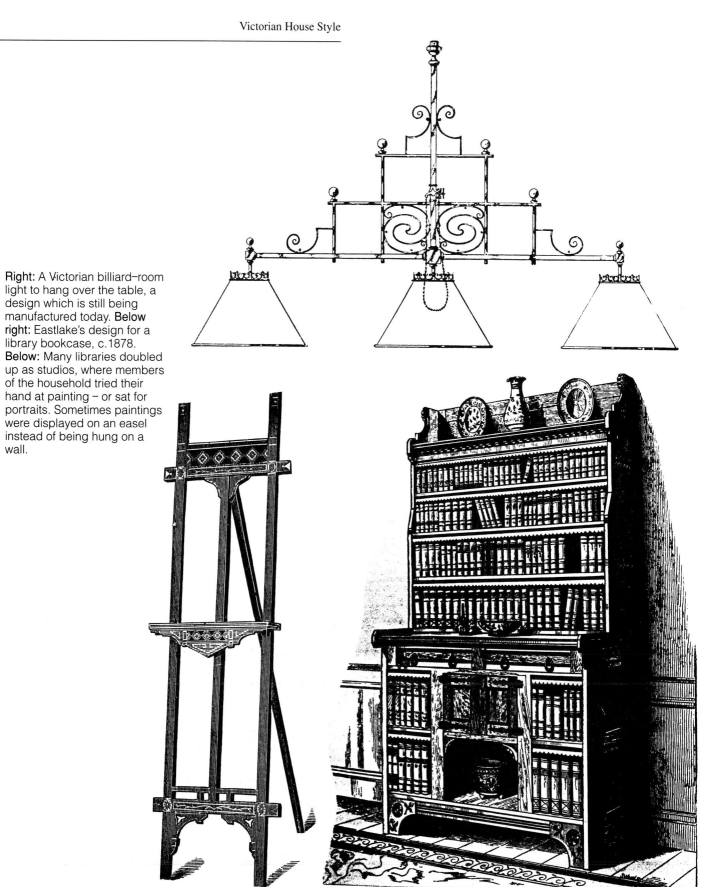

Right: A Victorian billiard–room light to hang over the table, a design which is still being manufactured today. **Below right:** Eastlake's design for a library bookcase, c.1878. **Below:** Many libraries doubled up as studios, where members of the household tried their hand at painting – or sat for portraits. Sometimes paintings were displayed on an easel instead of being hung on a wall.

Left: Two late–Victorian bookstands. Below left: An 1880 design for the arrangement and decoration of a library. Below: Architect R. W. Edis's design for a dining–room chimneypiece, 1880.

Chapter 4
Kitchens and Bathrooms

'It must be remembered that [the kitchen] is the great laboratory of every household, and that much of the "weal and woe" as far as regards bodily health depends upon the nature of the preparations concocted within its walls.'

Mrs Beeton

A modern kitchen can be given a period feel just by adding a cooking range. New Agas are available as are many original fittings, which can be reconditioned.
Robinson & Cornish. Holden Heat plc.

In today's world restoring a kitchen to its original Victorian state would, for most people, be impractical. We have become accustomed to modern, labour-saving appliances, which most of us would be loath to dispense with for the sake of authenticity. The skill therefore is in recreating the atmosphere of the Victorian kitchen whilst not sacrificing twentieth-century standards of hygiene and convenience.

In upper- and middle-class households, the Victorian kitchen was the domain of the servants. The lady of the house would supervise her staff, plan menus and check on the accounts, but the kitchen was, on the whole, 'out of bounds' to the family. Today the kitchen as family room, where cooking, eating and family activities occur, would have been anathema to most Victorians. Only poor, working-class families lived, cooked and ate in the same place because they could only afford to heat one room; a separate kitchen, therefore, would have been out of the question and the cooking was done over the open fire in the living room.

In most nineteenth-century houses, the kitchen was situated 'sufficiently remote from the principal apartments of the house, that the members, visitors, or guests of the family may not perceive the odour incident to cooking or hear the noise of culinary operations' (Mrs Beeton). It also had to have separate access so that servants and tradesmen did not have to pass through the rest of the house. In the first half of the century, the kitchen was in the basement, where fire risks were minimised as well. However, with the development and mass production of safer stoves, the introduction of plumbing and gas in the 1870s, and the disappearance of

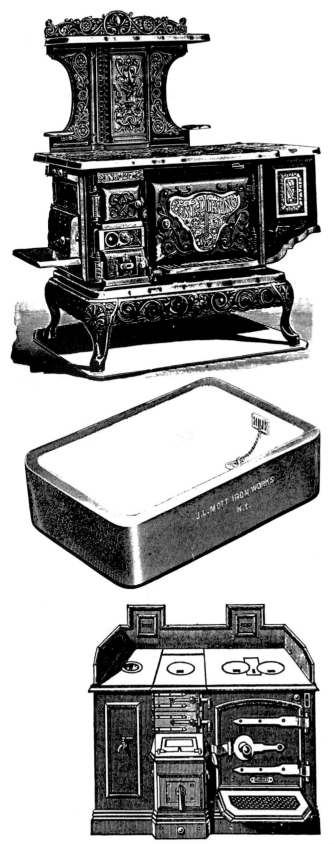

basements from the 1870s, kitchens became increasingly placed at the back of the house, usually in a rear extension.

Contrary to today's reproduction kitchen as an inviting, cosy room, the original Victorian kitchen was usually large and utilitarian, sited in an ill–lit and poorly ventilated part of the house, although Mrs Beeton listed 'excellence of light, height of ceiling and good ventilation' as one of the prerequisites necessary when erecting the kitchen. Any feeling of warmth was conveyed by the cooking range and the obligatory wooden dresser, which was packed with plates, dishes, spice boxes, jars and utensils. The only other furniture would have been a scrubbed wooden table on which food was prepared in the centre of the room, a heavy iron gas chandelier hanging above it, and a couple of simple chairs.

The sink, made of white or brown glazed stoneware with a single cold tap and a wooden draining–board, was in the adjoining scullery. Here the 'dirty work' of the household was carried out: the washing up, the peeling of vegetables, the polishing of brass and silver, etc. Some sculleries had an additional open fireplace, which was used for boiling laundry, for jam making and as an extra fire when guests were being entertained.

There would also be a larder, where fresh provisions were stored, and an ice–house, either situated on a back porch or in an underground tank. This was used for preserving food until the first refrigerators – deep, insulated wooden cabinets filled with pieces of ice – came into use in the 1860s.

In larger houses there would also be a butler's pantry between the kitchen and the dining room. Here additional serving dishes, glassware and silver were kept and finishing touches could be made to the meal before it appeared on the table. The pantry also stopped any odours and heat from the kitchen reaching the dining room.

Most of today's kitchens however do not have these ancillary rooms attached to them and have to combine all these domestic functions in one place. Modern ovens, dish–washers, fridges and washing machines therefore have to blend in with any period fittings, but this can be achieved if these appliances are kept as simple and as functional as possible because, unlike the rest of the Victorian house, the kitchen area was not filled with ornate architectural details.

By the turn of the century, when there was an increased awareness of the importance of hygiene and new inventions altered the pattern of domestic life, resulting in fewer households employing staff, kitchen design underwent a great change. It became plainer, more streamlined and more clinical – a style which has predominated throughout most of the twentieth century and which has only recently been challenged.

However, whilst it is virtually impossible to recreate a Victorian kitchen faithfully, its 'feel' can be evoked through the use of the following decorative features.

A selection of late–Victorian closed stoves and scullery sinks. Jelly moulds, mangles and knife sharpeners were also essential kitchen utensils.

The Kitchen Range

From the late eighteenth century, cooking and heating were combined in a cast–iron range, which incorporated an open coal fire contained in a grate, a crane for suspending pots and kettles close to the fire, an oven for baking on one side of the fire, a tank for heating water on the other, and a hot plate. Roasting was done on spits in front of the fire as the temperature inside the oven was difficult to control. However, as stoves developed and flue mechanisms improved, thus regulating temperatures more evenly, ovens gradually began to be used for roasting as well.

In 1802 the first closed stove was patented by George Bodley and by the 1840s these stoves had come into general use. In them, the fire was enclosed beneath a hot plate and the hot gases were forced through flues to heat the oven and the hot–water tank rather than escaping up the chimney. This meant that not only was there greater fuel efficiency, as an air–tight stove contained the heat and did not need refuelling as frequently, but safety was increased as the danger of falling embers or sparks was diminished.

Below left: Victorian kitchens always had lots of china on display, but usually on the wooden dresser. Glass–fronted china and glass cabinets were in the butler's pantry, but modern kitchens have to combine all the functions of the ancillary rooms of the Victorian kitchen area into one. **Below:** Stained–glass panels, tiles inset into the stove area and the pale–green colour scheme recreate some of the features of a Victorian kitchen.
Robinson & Cornish. London Door Company.

Left: The original fireplace and cooking range in the kitchen of Como House in Melbourne, Australia, c.1860.
Below: A traditional white porcelain butler's sink with a plate rack overhead.
Robinson & Cornish

A range of small
kitchen shelves, stoves
and utensils that appeared in
late−Victorian catalogues.

With large supplies of cheap coal available through the growing railway network, coal superseded wood as the solid fuel used to run these stoves. Although gas was introduced in the 1850s – a gas stove made its first appearance at the 1851 Great Exhibition – it did not come into general use until later in the century.

In Europe, Scandinavia was in the forefront of stove production and design and in 1869 a Norwegian cooking stove based on a heat–storage system was introduced. This was the forerunner of the Aga, invented by Ðr Gustav Dalen in 1924, which has become the most popular range installed in Victorian–style kitchens today, providing both the atmosphere of an original stove and the efficiency of a modern oven.

Although Victorian cast–iron kitchen ranges can be found in salvage yards and antique shops, few survive in their original environment, having been ripped out to make way for more modern equipment many years ago. Many have been reconditioned and restored to good working order, so that they can be used for cooking, but most are best kept for additional heating or pure decoration. If they are to be used, it is advisable to call in an expert to check that they are installed properly.

When reintroducing a cast–iron range into a kitchen, care needs to be taken that the proportions of the stove complement the dimensions of the room and of the fireplace opening. Originally the kitchen would have had either an open fire or a closed stove, so an element of disharmony may appear if the stove is the wrong size or if it distorts the original features of the fireplace. However, if a new oven is being installed, the chimney breast can be used to house a modern gas or electric hob, which will fit effectively across it and can look very attractive.

The Kitchen Dresser
No Victorian kitchen was without a wooden dresser, usually the only item of fitted furniture in the room, which was either set in the alcove created by the chimney breast or ranged along one wall. Here china was displayed on narrow shelves, with hooks for hanging cups and jugs on. Drawers would hold table linen and some utensils, and deep cupboards or a large open shelf underneath would store bulkier items such as bread bins, storage jars and pots not kept over the stove. These dressers were normally made of oak or painted deal, their colours being traditionally chocolate brown or bottle green.

Glass–fronted cabinets with panelled cupboards below were built in the butler's pantry and these found their way into some kitchens in late Victorian times.

When recreating a Victorian–style kitchen, there are many options on offer today. Junk and antique shops and salvage yards are full of old dressers, corner cupboards, wall cupboards, ventilated food cupboards, sideboards and plate racks, which can be used together to achieve the desired effect. These are often of stripped pine, which can then either be polished and left in their natural state or painted. Old library shelves can also provide

attractive open storage. Crammed with crockery jars and utensils, everyday items can be interestingly displayed and with everything in easy reach.

An alternative to using original pieces of furniture is to commission joinery to your own requirements. In this way, distinctive architectural details found in other rooms can be reflected in the kitchen and can complement the overall look of the house. For example, detailed panelling and door mouldings can be copied on the fronts of kitchen cupboards.

However, many people still prefer to have a custom–built kitchen and most firms have a traditional–style design amongst their ranges. Other companies are now also starting to reproduce individual items of kitchen furniture which are designed to combine practicality and 'authenticity'.

Sinks

As we have already said, the sink was originally in the scullery where the washing up and laundry were done. Nowadays, therefore, the only way of looking vaguely authentic is to have a heavy, white enamel butler's sink instead of the normal stainless steel variety found in most homes. It is worth looking in catalogues for hospital sinks, etc., where some interesting variations on the traditional enamel sink can still be found. However, most of these do not accommodate modern appliances such as waste–disposal units, so if these are essential items in your kitchen then you will have to use a stainless steel sink and make it blend in as unobtrusively as possible.

In Victorian times much of the kitchen staffs' day was spent at the sink either washing up or doing the laundry; therefore it was important to site the sink underneath the window to give them air, light and, in some cases, a view. However, with the convenience of today's washing–up machines, the sink can be placed anywhere in the room, which gives more scope to the overall design of the kitchen. It can even be inserted into an old piece of furniture, such as the base of a wooden dresser.

Wooden draining boards and tiled or marbled surrounds give a traditional feel, as do brass taps – either original ones or reproduction, although the latter are more efficient. Wooden plate racks above the sink for drainage or just for storage and decoration are also an attractive feature.

Top right: By the end of the nineteenth century, kitchens and sculleries were tiled as concern for hygiene grew. The sink was traditionally sited under a window.
Right: The kitchen range at Standen, in West Sussex, designed by Philip Webb in 1894. *National Trust*

Above: Many modern firms reproduce the furniture found in a Victorian kitchen with their period–style custom–built units.
Left: *Original Style* Victorian picture tiles inset into a recess can provide an otherwise modern kitchen with a period feature. *Mark Wilkinson Design*

Below: Cast–iron ranges with open fires and a closed oven for baking were gradually replaced by the 1840s with the more efficient closed stove. Mrs Beeton illustrated the American stove, bottom right, in her *Book of Household Management*.

Opposite: Utensils that Mrs Beeton felt that no kitchen should be without.

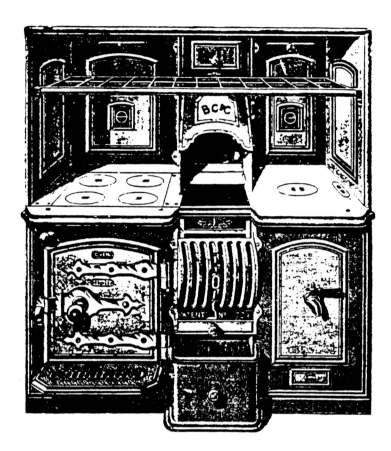

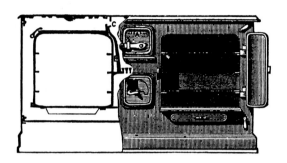

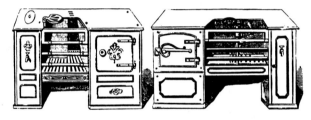

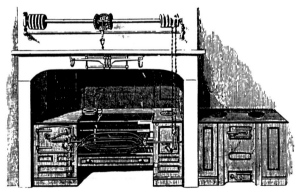

Tiles, Flooring and Wall Finishes

Original Victorian tiles for use around the sink or the oven can easily be found and look very effective, although complete sets are nowadays almost impossible to come across. Some tile manufacturers, however, now offer a wide variety of Victorian patterns, or else you can make an attractive patchwork of old tiles using complementary designs and colours.

Although the kitchen table was the only original work surface, nowadays most people prefer to keep the table for eating and provide work surfaces elsewhere in the room. These are best made out of a hardwood, such as teak, slate or tiles, but tiles can be difficult to keep clean as dirt can accumulate at the edges and in the grouting.

The flooring in Victorian kitchens would mostly have been of stone or hardwood – which was either oiled and then varnished or painted – which were easy to scrub clean. In the late nineteenth century a new, hard-wearing product, linoleum, became popular. It came in plain colours or patterns, was less slippery, and was cheap and hygienic. Whilst wood and linoleum are still in frequent use, quarry tiles, slate and cork tiles can provide an effective alternative form of flooring. Ceramic tiles were often placed around the base of the oven for safety reasons.

The walls were also painted, because they could be washed down or redecorated frequently, and were usually light in colour – cream or white. Painted furniture, such as the dresser, would then be in a different colour as we have described above. It is therefore easy to achieve a nostalgic feel just by using the same colour schemes.

The room had few architectural details: wainscoting or a tiled dado around it, and perhaps a plate rail about a foot below the ceiling for additional storage.

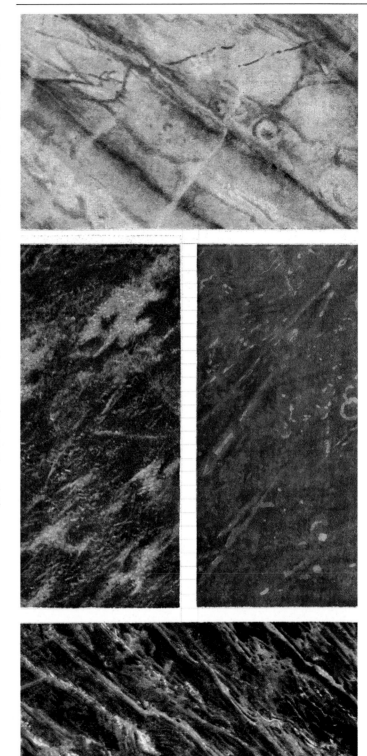

Opposite: Even if no longer functioning, a cast–iron range inset into a fireplace and surrounded by decorative tiles can conjure up the atmosphere of a nineteenth–century kitchen. *Original Style* English Delft tiles.
Right: Examples of *faux-*marbling widely used in Victorian times.

Right: Elaborate decoration found its way into the kitchen with ornate cast–iron stove backs and pretty, *papier - mâché* trays. **Below:** Hanging oil or gas lamps were placed in the centre of the room over the kitchen table. **Opposite:** Linoleum was the most popular type of flooring in the late–Victorian kitchen because it was durable and easy to keep clean. It was manufactured in a number of patterns, including imitation woods.

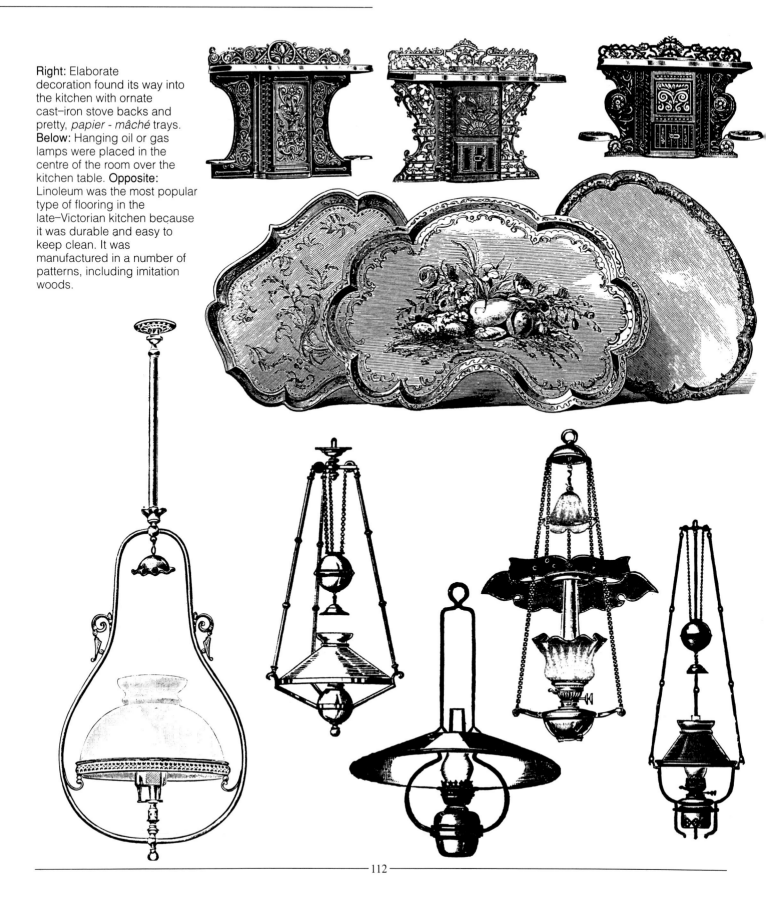

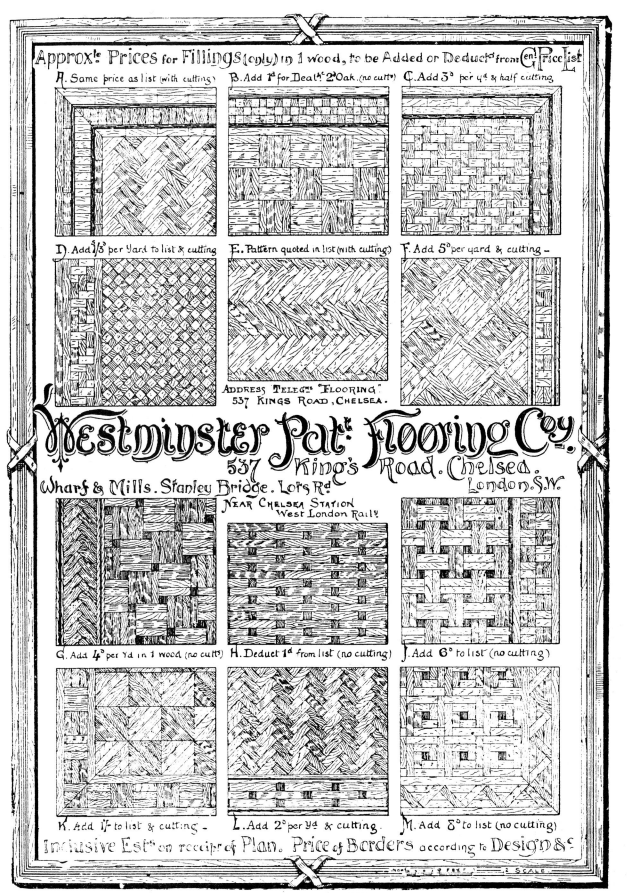

Approxᵗ Prices for Fillings (only) in 1 wood, to be Added or Deductᵈ from Genᵗ Price List

A. Same price as list (with cutting)
B. Add 1ᵈ for Deal (&c.) 2ᵈ Oak (no cutᵗʸ)
C. Add 3ᵈ per yᵈ & half cutting
D. Add 2/5 per Yard to list & cutting
E. Pattern quoted in list (with cutting)
F. Add 5ᵈ per yard & cutting

Address Telegᵗ "Flooring"
537 Kings Road, Chelsea.

Westminster Patᵗ Flooring Coy.
537 King's Road, Chelsea.
Wharf & Mills, Stanley Bridge, Lots Rᵈ
Near Chelsea Station
West London Railʸ
London, S.W.

G. Add 4ᵈ per Yd in 1 wood (no cutᵗˢ)
H. Deduct 1ᵈ from list (no cutting)
J. Add 6ᵈ to list (no cutting)
K. Add 1/- to list & cutting
L. Add 2ᵈ per Yᵈ & cutting
M. Add 8ᵈ to list (no cutting)

Inclusive Estˢ on receipt of Plan. Price of Borders according to Design &c

Bathrooms

Like the kitchen, the recreation of an exact Victorian bathroom is incompatible with today's sanitary needs. What one has to aim for, therefore, is an evocation of the spirit of the nineteenth century but with the use of mostly twentieth-century fittings.

Before 1870 most houses were built without bathrooms. People washed themselves in their bedrooms in front of a fire, with hot water brought upstairs by the servants. The most common forms of baths were shallow ones from which one could sponge oneself down; hip baths made of zinc or iron, which were usually painted dark brown on the outside and cream or marbled on the inside, and which were curved at the back and deep enough for most of the body to be submerged; Sitz baths, which were either oval or square with a small seat; and portable showers – a tent-like contraption with a water tank at its top from which water cascaded down on to the bather. The variety of designs available were well in evidence by the time of the 1851 Great Exhibition, when numerous types of baths – including very ornate French ones – were on display. Bedrooms were also equipped with washstands, shaving stands and chamber pots.

Two different ways of recreating a Victorian bathroom, but with modern, reproduction fittings. Gleaming brass, wood and antique accessories complete the scene.

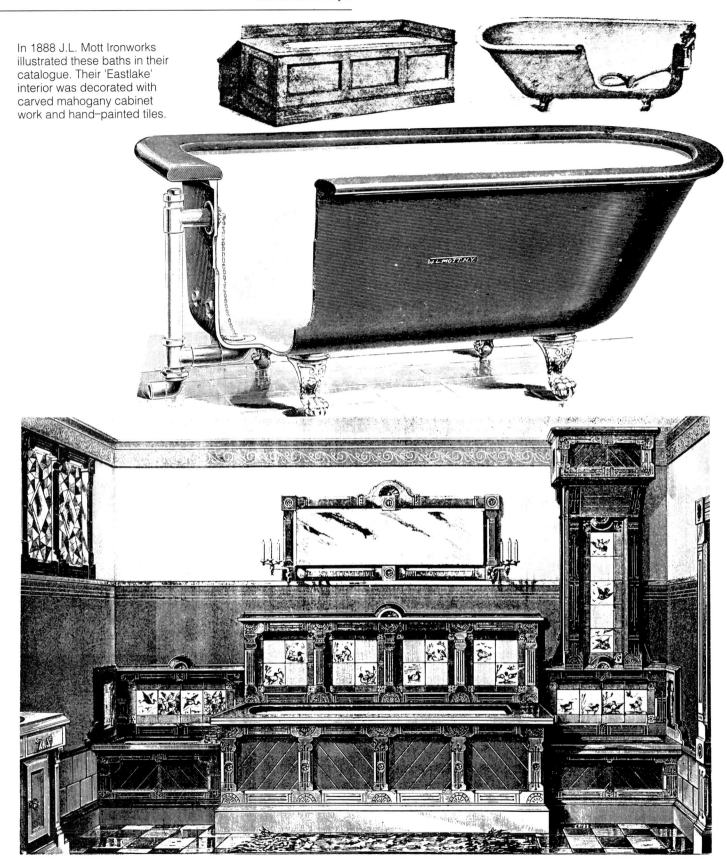

In 1888 J.L. Mott Ironworks illustrated these baths in their catalogue. Their 'Eastlake' interior was decorated with carved mahogany cabinet work and hand-painted tiles.

However, the development of a circulatory hot–water system piping water around the house, the invention of a 'wash–out' water closet in 1875 and improvements in the overall sewage and drainage systems, coupled with the new concern for hygiene and cleanliness in the later part of the nineteenth century, meant that the fixed bathroom became a feature of the late Victorian home. These soon became status symbols as few houses had more than one bathroom, and washstands in the bedrooms remained in use until well into the turn of the century.

To begin with bathrooms were converted from bedrooms and dressing rooms and thus retained a feeling of cosiness and space. The architectural details in the room echoed those in the rest of the house: ornamental mouldings on the ceilings and cornices, wooden floors, stained–glass window panels and simple fireplaces for both warmth and ventilation. Toilets, basins and bath tubs were encased in wooden pieces of furniture to hide their function, to conceal ugly pipes and to make the room resemble any other in the house. Other decorative items completed the scene: rush– or cane–seated chairs, wooden towel rails, Oriental rugs, small tables crammed with toiletries, pictures, prints, mahogany–framed mirrors and washstands transported from the bedroom. Dark, strongly patterned wallpapers were often used to decorate the room as they hid any stains from condensation and splashmarks. Pretty, gathered curtains covered the windows.

As concern for health grew towards the end of the century, bathrooms took on more hygienic forms. To counteract hidden germs, tiled floors and dados, and exposed pipes and sanitary fittings became standard features because they could be kept clean more easily. Bathrooms became smaller and more streamlined as they began to be purpose–built, and by the beginning of the twentieth century a style had been adopted that closely resembles the modern bathroom of today.

The portable cast–iron baths described above were replaced by fixed baths after 1870, when it became possible to heat a water tank on an upper storey via the kitchen range below so that hot water could be piped throughout the house. Cast–iron baths, coated inside with white porcelain enamel, were initially encased in wood–panelled surrounds with tiled splashbacks around the top. This prevented the enamel from chipping as well as hiding unsightly pipes. However, as hygiene became increasingly important in the 1880s, tubs began to be free–standing, with rolled tops and claw or ball feet, so that they could be washed underneath. For decoration, they were often painted or stencilled with floral patterns. Pipes were left exposed, which enabled regular polishing; their gleaming brass and copper exteriors provided the room with an additional feature.

Although washstands with jugs and bowls were still to be found in many bedrooms, fixed ceramic basins – or lavatories, as they were called – soon appeared in the bathroom. At first these were set in marble–topped washstands or in varnished mahogany cabinets, again

From the 1880's needle and spray showers became commercially available.

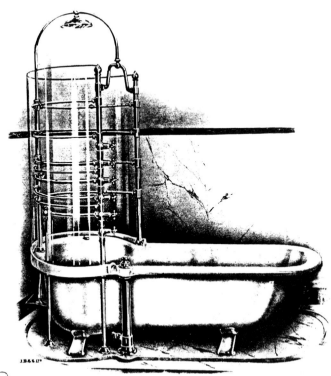

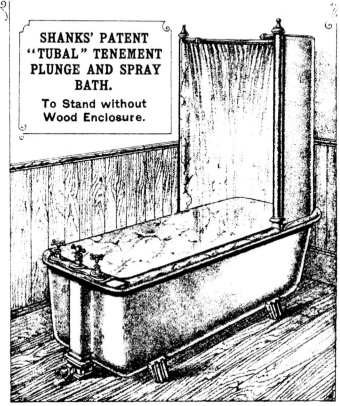

SHANKS' PATENT "TUBAL" TENEMENT PLUNGE AND SPRAY BATH.

To Stand without Wood Enclosure.

with the pipes concealed. Later, however, for reasons of hygiene, they began to be suspended from ornamental iron brackets or supported by metal legs, with their plumbing on view underneath. With splashbacks of patterned tiles or marble, these basins often had designs inside to match those of the bath. By the end of the century, plain ceramic ware and pedestal bases, for example in the shape of a neo–classical column, became the fashion as more functional lines were adopted.

Fitted taps of brass, nickel or porcelain, with either lever or cross–shaped handles, added the finishing touch.

Fixed showers were another late–Victorian invention. Most just had a wide, brass showerhead, but some also had 'needle' sprays, which projected invigorating streams of water from circular pipes at different levels of the body.

Nowadays, original Victorian baths and basins can still be found in salvage yards and specialist antique shops, but they tend to be more expensive than their modern counterparts as demand exceeds supply due to the destruction of many original fittings. If in poor condition, the interior of a cast–iron bath can be recoated with bath enamel and fitted with new brass taps. However, effective reproductions of Victorian styles are available from most bathroom manufacturers, although new roll–top baths are shorter than their predecessors. Reproduction brass taps are also widely manufactured, although original ones are easy to find; however, the Victorian ones may be too furred up to be efficient and will also require frequent polishing. Without domestic help to do this, it is probably more sensible to settle for today's brass–plated versions. Another equally effective alternative is to install simple, white modern fittings with new, brass–plated taps, or a white bath encased in plain dark–wood panelling, and to achieve a period look with other decorative touches.

Opposite and left: Before the 1880s washstands were hidden in marble–topped mahogany cabinets. However, with increased interest in hygiene, fittings began to be exposed so that they can be cleaned easily. Original washstands can still be found in antique shops and then plumbed with modern fixtures.
Above left: The simple addition of brass taps and a flower–painted basin can provide a modern bathroom with Victorian details. *Pipe Dreams*

The Water Closet

The first flushing lavatory was invented in 1596, but the precursor of the Victorian water closet was not introduced until 1778, when Joseph Bramah developed a system with a pan, closed at the bottom by a valve, and a handle which, when pulled, operated a series of levers that opened the valve, poured in water from an upper bowl to flush through the contents and then closed the valve again. The top bowl would then be refilled automatically. As this method was complicated and therefore expensive, as well as using up a great deal of water, the Bramah water closet originally appeared only in wealthier homes, with the cheaper Hopper water closet being in more common use. This consisted of a funnel with a U–bend trap, and later an S–bend version, into which water was poured through a hole in the side which swirled the contents through the trap and into a drainpipe. However, as only one in ten houses in London was linked to a proper sewer in 1855, with drainage and sewage disposal varying from town to town, few homes had indoor facilities until the middle of the century. Outside privies with a cesspit placed under the toilet, earth closets with dry earth or ashes underneath instead of flushing water, and chamber pots emptied by servants were the norm, with sewage disposed of by 'night soil men'.

By the middle of the century plumbing improved with the development of cast iron or glazed earthenware pipes, and by the 1870s better sewage systems had been installed. Improvements in supplying more houses with water, as well as in piping water round the house, also led to better sanitary arrangements inside the home, and by 1880 most new houses were built with a water closet. The introduction of overhead water storage tanks allowed waste to be flushed through the system by water rushing down to the pan from a raised cistern, which by 1890 had developed into the standard 'washdown' toilet which is still in use today. This system was pioneered by Thomas Crapper in his Chelsea works and soon superseded other types of water closet. The low–level cistern, based on the same principle, was introduced in 1895 and eventually became the most common type to be installed.

Initially inside toilets were in a separate room from the bathroom and were often hidden away in a space without ventilation. However, an Act of Parliament in 1875 regulated that they must have at least one outside wall with a window. They also had to have their own water supply and a separate soil pipe leading to a sewer.

As the installation of toilets increased, so their design improved. The Victorians' reticence about such matters meant that, at first, water closets were often disguised, with a wooden box built over the bowl or even an upholstered armchair. As awareness of hygiene led to simpler, exposed fittings in other areas, so toilets took on the form we know today. Manufactured mostly by Twyford and Doulton, they had glazed earthenware or porcelain bowls, frequently painted inside and out with flowers or landscapes, supported on pedestals

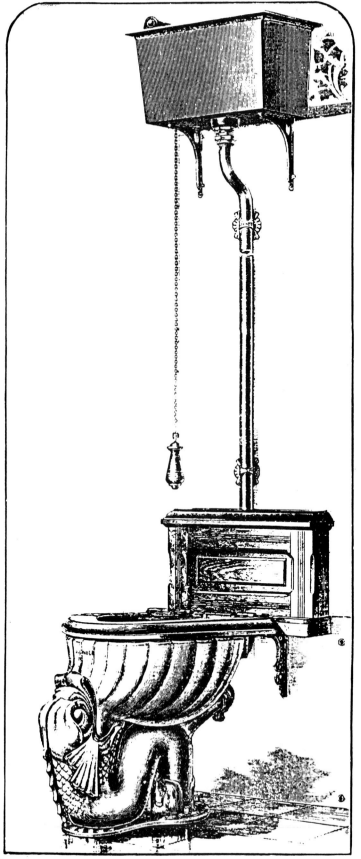

Opposite:'The Dolphin' water closet, 1888. **This page:** By the end of the nineteenth century bathroom walls were tiled, with co–ordinating patterned borders, cornices and dado–rails. Floors were also tiled and pipes were exposed. Interiors were plainer, but toilet bowls and bases were still targets for decoration.

sculpted in the shapes of crouching lions and dolphins. Polished walnut or mahogany seats (or pine in servants' toilets), supported on cast–iron brackets, and porcelain cisterns and handles completed the scene. However, by the turn of the century, toilet fittings had become plainer, echoing the more clinical lines of the new bathrooms being installed.

Whilst late–Victorian toilet bowls and cisterns can still be found and plumbed in to modern pipework, many firms have begun to reproduce original styles and decorative patterns, thus providing late–twentieth–century standards of sanitation with a period look. A Victorian 'feel' can also be achieved by just adding a polished wooden seat – either old or new – to a simple, modern toilet.

Below: Stained–glass windows, original overmantel and wooden details can give a small bathroom or cloakroom a Victorian 'feel'. **Below right:** A tiled tripartite wall. **Opposite:** A pretty evocation of a Victorian–style bathroom.
BC Sanitan Pipe Dreams

Tiles, Flooring and Other Decorative Details

As the demand for better hygiene grew, and as smaller purpose-built bathrooms became standard features in new housing, so the highly decorated, furniture-laden bathroom began to disappear. Tiles replaced wallpaper and wooden floors so that bathrooms could be kept clean more easily. Deep dados with plain or embossed tiles in rich colours, co-ordinating floor tiles and picturesque friezes became standard features, with complementary designs and colours around the sinks and bath-tubs. Gradually tilework became less decorated, with plainer dados bordered by a simple patterned tile.

Although tiles began to be mass produced to meet the new demand, they were still expensive. Cheaper alternatives, which were equally washable, were linoleum for floors and anaglypta paper for walls.

Windows, which were originally covered with gathered curtains to complement the other elaborate features in the room, also adopted a simpler style and fussy drapes were replaced with shutters, wooden Venetian blinds or a plain curtain. However, many bathroom windows also had richly coloured stained-glass panels in them.

Modern bathrooms can acquire a Victorian look in a number of ways, therefore. With or without original or reproduction fittings, a period mood can be created in a large bathroom simply by the addition of furniture. Mahogany or scrubbed pine washstands; wooden armoires and free-standing towel rails; chairs and tables; antique mirrors in ornate wooden frames, pictures and prints; small Victorian chandeliers or wall sconces; floral-patterned wallpapers and fabrics; wooden floors, covered with Oriental or rag rugs or painted with stencilled borders; stained-glass panels in windows; and gleaming brass accessories – all help to conjure up a nostalgic atmosphere. In a small, more functional bathroom with modern fittings, a wooden toilet seat, dark wooden panelling around the bath and a few of the above extras can be equally effective.

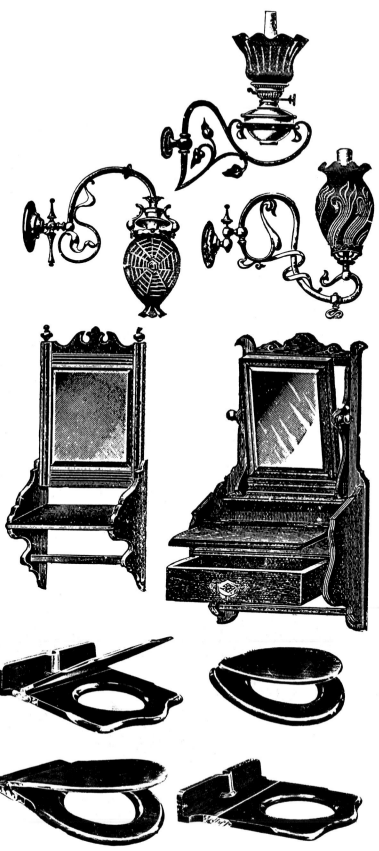

Some of the bathroom accessories available from late - Victorian catalogues.

Chapter 5
Interior Details

'… a Gentleman's House ought to be not merely substantial, comfortable, convenient and well furnished, but fairly adorned.'

Robert Kerr, The Gentleman's House (1864)

Whilst the internal rooms of the house were architecturally simple – mainly rectangular in shape with a projecting window bay – the interior details which were part of the main fabric of the house echoed the elaborate ornamentation so beloved elsewhere by the Victorians. Dados, cornices, ceilings, doors, floors and woodwork all displayed elements of decoration, varying in degrees of elaborateness depending on the status of the occupants, but nevertheless still in evidence even in a lower–class house. As Robert Kerr wrote in 1864, 'A Gentleman's House … whilst it ought to be free of ostentation, ought to be equally free of the opposite extreme.…If we see stately entertainments conducted with all the manifestations of wealth, with the aids of choice and valuable furniture and plate, paintings and perhaps sculpture, in rooms whose walls and ceilings are helplessly devoid of decoration, the contrast is absurd.' The art was to achieve grace and elegance through moderation: 'no exuberance, but no poverty'.

Walls

At the beginning of the Victorian era, the walls of a room were treated as one with the cornice at the top and the skirting board at the bottom, although in tall rooms the use of dados began to be advocated in the late 1830s. J. C. Loudon, in 1838, recommended installing a false dado in a high–ceilinged room by applying a chair rail to the walls and painting the area in between the rail and the skirting board. Picture rails were also added about three–quarters of the way to the ceiling in order to break up a large expanse of wall.

Skirting boards were kept plain throughout, with unornamented mouldings that were either painted (often in dark colours such as maroon or brown), grained to look like wood or marbleised. They were about twelve

To recreate the feel of an authentic Victorian home it is important to remember their love of elaborate decoration which they applied to every available surface.

inches high and an inch and a half thick, protruding from the wall to protect the wallpaper.

However, the dado – three to four feet in height and built out from the wall – became increasingly popular and by the 1870s, Charles Eastlake in his *Hints on Household Taste* was advocating the division of the wall into three areas: the dado, the frieze or cornice around the top, and the central filling in between. Instead of the dado, the bottom part of the wall could have wainscoting or be papered in a different pattern to the central area. Each section of the wall was treated as a separate entity and decorated accordingly. This then became the standard approach to walls for the 1880s and 1890s.

Wood panelling for the lower section of the wall was very expensive and therefore only appeared in wealthier homes or in a main reception room, although ready –made wainscoting, which simulated panelling, soon became available.

Dados were particularly used in hallways or dining rooms, where they protected the plastering on the walls from chair backs and from people rushing through the hall. These would be treated in a variety of ways. Larger houses used an embossed paper with a surface resembling leather which came in a number of patterns, including exotic birds, flowers, fruit and the newly fashionable Japanese designs, a cheaper substitute was a canvas which looked like mock leather. Washable, varnished and embossed papers like anaglypta and Lincrusta (see page 66) were the most popular for dados, although ceramic tiles were frequently used for entrance halls, staircases and corridors. Made from glazed bricks or faience, tiles with a glossier surface due to an additional firing, the most usual colours for them were peacock blue, ochre and green.

The central area of the wall was then decorated, usually with densely patterned wallpapers.

The cornice or frieze then completed the wall, joining it with the ceiling. Decorative friezes, complementing the wallpaper in a co–ordinating pattern or colour, or highly decorated plaster cornices adorned the main rooms of the house, with simpler patterns in the bedrooms. Originally hand–carved, with the develop–ment of fibrous plaster (ordinary plaster strengthened with coarse canvas) it was easier to mass produce whole lengths of cornicing – with elaborate designs of foliage and flowers, fluting, classical Greek motifs and scrollwork. It was also cheaper to install, which meant that most houses could afford to have intricately moulded plasterwork. These cornices would then be painted, sometimes in several colours.

Where this moulded plasterwork still remains, the delicate patterns are often disfigured by successive layers of paint; however these details can be restored with patient cleaning. Although cornicing is very frequently damaged or lost, fibreglass and plaster reproductions are now available in a variety of original motifs.

The tripartite wall was less fashionable in the last

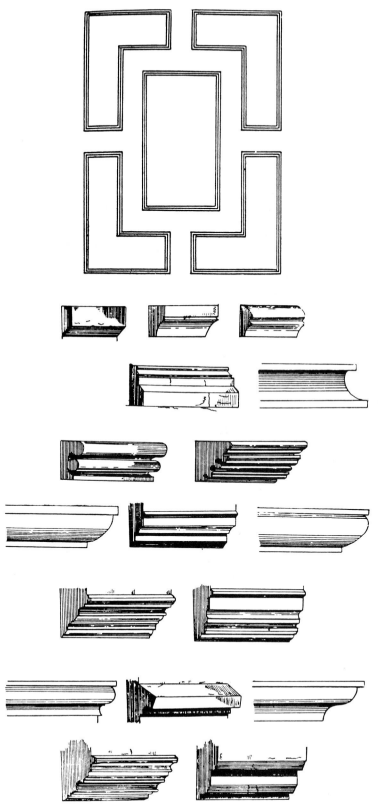

decade of the nineteenth century, with dados becoming higher and friezes and cornices deeper – between three to four feet down from the ceiling – and only a narrow central band to be wallpapered. As designs got simpler, there would either be a dado or a frieze, but not both. The emphasis shifted from the horizontal at the turn of the century when exponents of the Art Nouveau movement began dividing the wall vertically with the use of columns and pilasters.

An alternative to the tripartite wall was wood panelling, but this was very expensive because of the cost of hardwoods like oak. However, softwoods grained to look like mahogany and oak were often used instead. As the overall effect was heavy and dark, wood–panelled rooms were rarely found except in grand entrance halls or libraries. Full–height panelling, stained and varnished, became a feature of some Gothic Revival homes, whilst small, painted panels – in white or a light colour – covering three–quarters of the wall were popular in Queen Anne Revival houses later in the century.

Opposite: Wall panelling was often inset with patterned wallpaper or trompe l'oeil decoration. **Left:** Towards the end of the Victorian era, it was no longer fashionable for walls to be divided into three sections. One alternative style was floor–to–ceiling wall panels, decorated with heavily patterned wallpaper and edged with a narrow skirting board and cornice. **Below:** Full–height wall panelling was often to be found in the masculine rooms of the house – the library or the billiard room. However, as hardwoods were very expensive, grained softwoods or simulated wood papers were frequently used instead. *Astonleigh Studio*

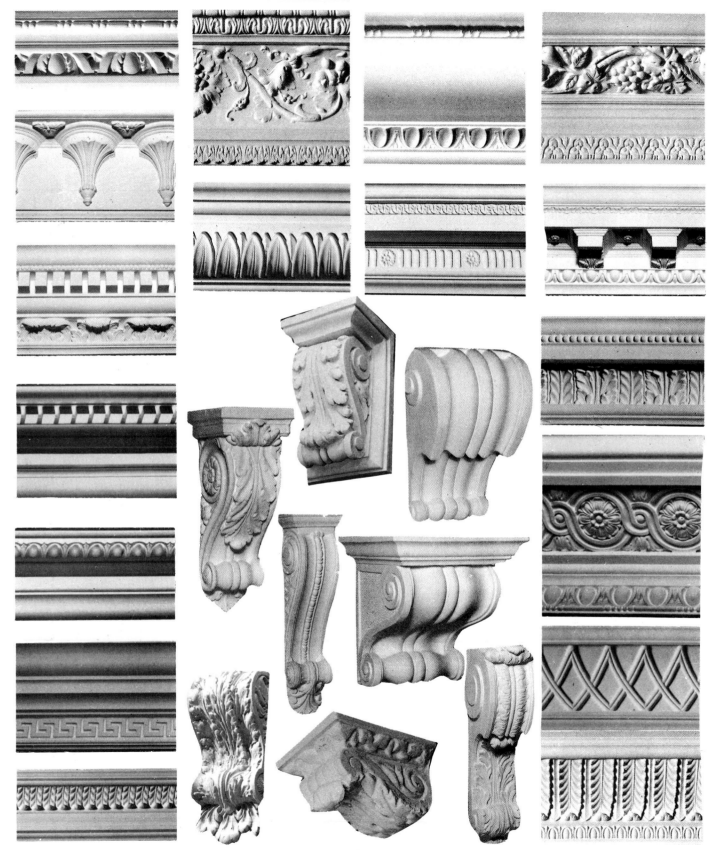

Ceilings

Even in a modest Victorian house, the main rooms had high ceilings, with an ornate ceiling rose or medallion in the centre. Originally made of hand–carved plasterwork, or papier mâché, these became standard fixtures when fibrous plaster allowed cheaper ceiling decorations to be commercially mass produced. Where there was a central light fitting – a chandelier or a hanging gas/oil lamp – the ceiling rose circled the mount of the light. In the early Victorian era it was usually no more than two feet in diameter, becoming larger later in the century. However, the size and elaborateness of the rose was determined by the importance of the room. Ornate mouldings were carved in a variety of designs, echoing those of the cornices: flowers and foliage, scrollwork, classical Greek motifs and fluting. Elaborate ceiling friezes were additional features, as were corner decorations such as urns, acanthus leaves and garlands of flowers.

With the development of the Arts and Crafts movement, ceilings became lower so as to create a cosier effect in a room. A mock Gothic vaulted look was achieved by the use of ribbed and moulded beams, and in late Victorian times half–timbered ceilings with exposed beams became fashionable.

From the 1880s ceilings were covered with a number of finishes: light–weight anaglypta paper; painted pressed tin – popular in the United States for kitchens and

Once fibrous plaster became commercially available, decorative cornices, friezes, ceiling medallions and brackets began to appear on the walls and ceilings of most Victorian rooms. Designs ranged from classical motifs in intricately moulded floral patterns.

bathrooms; ceiling papers which imitated frescoes and painted scenes; ordinary papers complementing those on the walls, often with a circular repeating pattern around the ceiling rose; or canvas paper on which stencilled designs could appear. Whilst earlier in the century ceilings were usually painted in a light colour, with a second colour highlighting certain details, by the late Victorian era heavier and more numerous colours were used along with highly patterned ceiling papers.

Right: The design of the ceiling rose was normally a single flower with stylised petals spread out around it. If the room was lit by a chandelier, the centre of the ceiling rose would circle its mount. **Below:** The Victorians' love of decoration extended to their ceilings with the use of heavily carved and gilded friezes.

Left: This dado and Victorian cast–iron radiator are painted in a traditional burgundy colour. The dado border is a Greek key pattern.**Below:** Victorian bookshelves were often built in a classical style, with pediments and pilasters. The lavish drapes with several layers of different fabric treatment are typical of High Victorian style.

Internal Doors

Doors inside the house were either panelled or, in simpler homes, of tongue and grooved boards. In wealthier homes, the doors would be made of a hardwood such as oak, usually with four panels; however, as hardwood was expensive, softwood was often used instead, either grained to look like hardwood or painted in a dark 'wood' colour. The internal doors reflected the style of the rest of the house, for example, Gothic homes had pointed, arched doors and Italianate buildings rounded, arched ones. The doors of the most important rooms in the house would then be framed by imposing architraves with classical columns or beautiful carving.

Decorative glass panels were normally found inset in hall, kitchen and bathroom doors, either of coloured, patterned stained glass, or of plain glass with an etched or painted design. Door panels were also decorated with stencils, painted scenes and patterned wallpaper.

Door furniture was usually of gleaming brass, with elegant handles, elaborate escutcheons and finger plates in the varying styles of the period. Painted porcelain or plain china finger plates and door knobs were also popular.

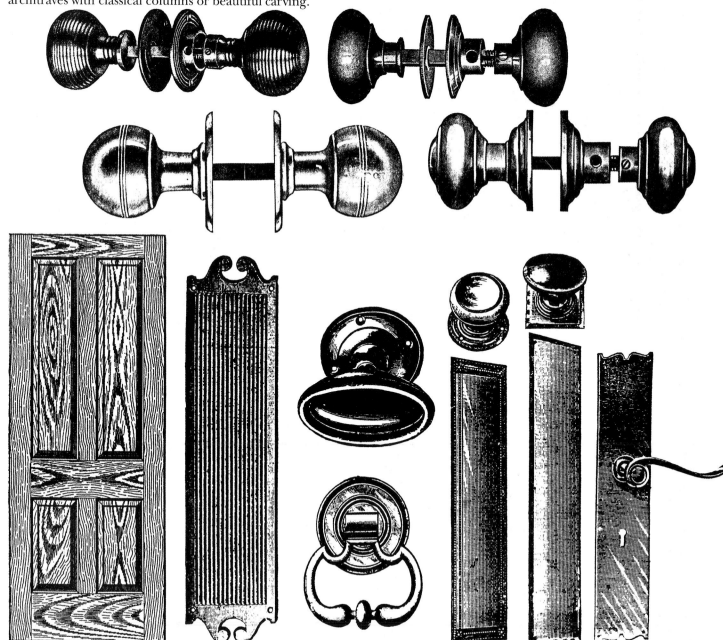

A simple panelled door would then be embellished with brass door furniture, decorated panels and elaborate door frames.

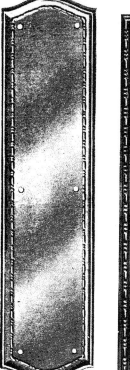

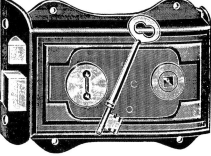

Two very extreme door treatments, with grained and stencilled panels, ornate brass door furniture and heavily draped *portières*.

Interior Decoration

William Morris's bold designs for wallpapers, curtains, upholstery fabrics and carpets characterise the style of interior decoration most associated with the Victorian era: strong, floral and naturalistic patterns in deep, rich colours. However, this High Victorian look was really only fashionable from the 1850s until the late 1880s, with lighter, simpler forms of decor predominating at the beginning and end of Victoria's reign.

Until the middle of the nineteenth century, the classical styles of the Regency period were still in evidence and the main reception rooms were decorated in pale, elegant colours, with cream, lavender, pearl grey, light green, pale pink and blue being the most popular. With the improvement in chemical dyes in the 1850s and the development of the wallpaper industry, stronger colours – for example, plum, sage green, Prussian blue and gold – and complex patterns could now be achieved and were quickly adopted in most homes. Only bedrooms were kept light and simple. Upholstery and curtains also reflected the new fashion for over-decoration by becoming fussier and more elaborately draped and trimmed. It was not until the 1890s that plain white or cream colour schemes and simpler decorative styles were back in favour, revived by the Arts and Crafts movement.

Wallpapers

Until wallpapers began to be mass produced in the 1840s, walls were usually painted and enlivened with a decorative border, marbled, grained to look like wood or stencilled. Wealthier homes also hung strips of printed damask, watered silk or cotton on their walls or on the inside of panelling, but these fabric wall coverings were very expensive. However, with the development of the technique of printing from engraved cylinders on to rolls of paper in the early 1840s, interior wall decoration was revolutionised. Rolls of wallpaper began to be commercially produced – resulting in lower costs and a wider choice of designs – and soon adorned the walls of most Victorian households.

Wallpapers began to be manufactured in a variety of finishes from plain papers with simple patterns on them to finer quality satin papers and elaborately decorated flock papers. Early designs included flowers, plants, trellis-work, birds, animals, and French-inspired three-dimensional pictorial scenes of landscapes and historical events. Deep wallpaper borders of about three inches were also fashionable with patterns of flowers, trailing vines, Greek urns and acanthus leaves. But it was Owen Jones's *The Grammar of Ornament*, published in 1856, with its colour illustrations of ornamentation around the world, which had the most initial influence on wallpaper patterns. Gothic, Moorish, Oriental and classical motifs soon appeared on wallpapers, as did the diaper (diamond) motif used by Pugin on his wallpaper designs for the Houses of Parliament. After the publication of Charles Eastlake's book, *Hints on Household Taste*, in 1878,

three-dimensional scenes were abandoned in favour of 'walls [that] should at all times be flat', with 'the very appearance of rotundity avoided'.

However, it was William Morris who had the most profound effect on wallpaper design. His flat, rhythmical patterns, hand-printed by his company Morris, Marshall Faulkner and Co. (later Morris and Co.), were based on medieval motifs and on nature – his earliest papers, 'Daisy', 'Fruit' and 'Trellis', were inspired by the flowers and fruit found in his garden at The Red House – and between 1862 and 1896 the Company produced a large range of sweeping, naturalistic patterns in warm, subtle colours achieved by using traditional vegetable dyes instead of the new chemical methods. These included sage greens, rusts, peacock blue and gold. Patterns inspired by Renaissance tapestries were also popular, especially for dining rooms, and Morris himself hung original tapestries on his walls, although these were out of the financial reach of most households. His designs were widely adopted and by 1882 one author was noting that a majority of the Aesthetes living in Norman Shaw's Bedford Park estate had 'the wallpapers and designs of Morris'. Most of his designs are still available today.

The tripartite wall had also become fashionable in the 1870s, with dados covered in the new embossed papers. Lincrusta, introduced in 1877, was a thick relief paper which imitated stamped Spanish leather, whilst anaglypta was a lighter, more flexible paper, which was either painted dark brown to simulate leather, or embossed with Oriental, flower, fruit or bird motifs and then painted. The area in between the dado and the cornice was filled with a patterned wallpaper, often a William Morris design.

Only in the bedroom were thinner papers used, decorated with lightly patterned bird, flower and ribbon designs.

Opposite: An early advertisement for Lincrusta, which was first available in 1877.

Right: William Morris's 'Willow Boughs' wallpaper design, first produced in the 1890s.
Below: His 'Wallflower' design, a pattern of decorative, curvaceous forms, was first produced in 1890.

The Arts and Crafts and the Aesthetic movements decorated their walls with deep-patterned friezes and borders.

The simpler styles of the Arts and Crafts movement in the last decade of the nineteenth century led to wallpaper patterns becoming less intense, with those by C.F.A. Voysey being the most influential. Flowers, fruit, birds and foliage were still the main motifs, but in more delicate forms and with lighter backgrounds. Imported Japanese grass papers and Chinese designs were also in vogue. With the disappearance of the tripartite wall, deep decorative frieze papers began to be produced, designed by artists like Walter Crane. However, many Arts and Crafts homes did not have wallpaper at all, preferring to leave walls either plain white or of painted wood panelling.

Curtains and Upholstery

Victorian homes were renowned for the lavishness of their curtains and the fussiness of their upholstery treatments. The recently developed Jacquard loom, which allowed the design to be incorporated into the weave, meant that popular wallpaper patterns, such as birds, flowers and trellis–work, could also appear on furnishing fabrics. Initially, favourite colours were crimson and bottle green, but by the 1860s improved chemical dyes led to brighter colours like yellow, green and Prussian blue becoming available. William Morris also successfully produced a wide range of fabrics in the same patterns as his wallpapers.

As we have already noted, windows were often dressed with four layers of curtains. These were not only to provide decoration but to protect the room from the harmful rays of the sun; however, this resulted in dark, airless rooms, as the main source of light and ventilation was hidden behind a vast amount of material. The simple muslin or net 'glass curtain', next to the window, would be underneath a lace or muslin curtain, or a festooned blind. On top would be a heavily draped silk, damask, figured satin, velvet, worsted or moreen curtain, trimmed with fringes, tassels, brocades and ribbons, and framed with an elaborately shaped valance (lambrequin), which sometimes almost reached the floor on either side and extended down to about one–third of the curtain at the centre. A boxed–in cornice contained the pole from which the valance and the main curtain hung, but if there was no cornice, the valance would then be draped around the pole. Curtains were also over–long so that they could be looped back during the day with sumptuous tie–backs.

Window treatments were simpler in bedrooms, where lighter fabrics – chintzes, cretonnes and cotelans – were used. In the summer, heavy drapes were taken down around the house and replaced with thinner, muslin or cotton curtains.

By the late 1870s, Charles Eastlake was calling for simple window arrangements, with no 'heavy and artificial folds'. Complaining about the fashion for over–elaborate drapery, he felt that curtains should hang straight from a wooden or brass pole to about two or three inches above the floor. However, this style was not adopted until later in the century, when the Queen Anne Revival and Arts and Crafts movements advocated having plain curtains with simple tie–backs.

Roller blinds and wooden Venetian blinds were also a feature of Victorian windows and were placed under the main curtain. Roller blinds, fitted next to the window, would often be painted with landscapes or printed with geometric and arabesque patterns, and then trimmed with fringes. But towards the end of the nineteenth century, with the renewed fashion for simplicity, plain, shiny white taffeta or buff–coloured blinds were more often to be found. Some windows also had wooden shutters underneath all the layers of drapery.

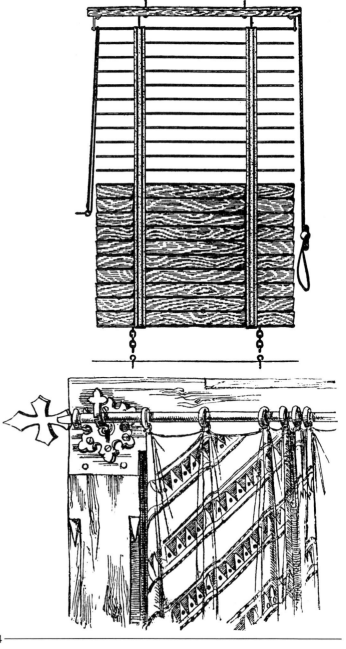

Wooden Venetian blinds and shutters were often to be found on Victorian windows. In the High Victorian era, they were then covered with several layers of curtaining. However, in 1878 Eastlake was decrying this fashion and advocating simple arrangements for curtains and *portières* (below).

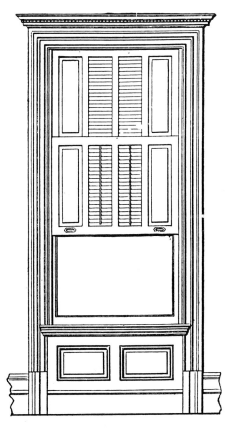

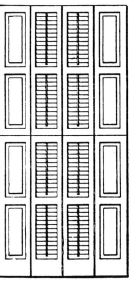

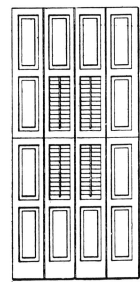

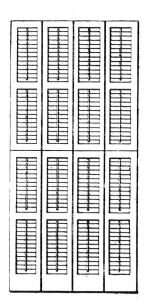

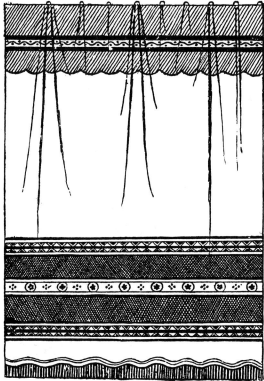

The pale, lightly patterned silk and chintz upholstery covering the classical–styled furniture of the 1840s soon gave way to the deep buttoning and rich decoration which is synonymous with Victoriana. Deep buttoning was made possible by the invention of the coil spring in the 1850s, and soon Victorian homes were filled with heavily stuffed sofas, chairs and chaises, covered with velvet, boldly patterned wools, damask, or 'rep' (a cord finish), and then trimmed with lavish fringing, brocade and tassels. Even chair legs were draped with festoons of material and fancy trimmings. Tapestry, velvet or needlework cushions, also with elaborate borders, were then scattered on top. This over–dressed look was then completed with muslin or lace anti–macassars.

William Morris's densely patterned fabrics were also widely used to upholster furniture, as were floral chintzes and cretonnes, stamped leather, imitation tapestries and needlework. By the end of the century, however, furnishing fabrics had become plainer, with stamped leather, lightly printed velvets and cretonnes, and hand–woven materials being more fashionable.

Elaborate drapes and ruched
pelmets evoke the atmosphere
of a Victorian drawing room.
*Lighting Designs Ltd. Osborne
& Little plc.*

Flooring

With improvements in methods of machine–weaving, the average Victorian family could afford to have carpet in its main reception rooms. In 1838, Loudon was advocating the use of Brussels carpeting (with a heavy pile formed by uncut loops of wool), although he felt that 'Axminster carpet, thick and without a seam, is the most splendid article of the sort in England'. *Cassell's Household Guide* also recommended the more hard–wearing Kidderminster carpet, which, however, was 'rarely suitable for parlours, the green moss or small green–and–black coral pattern excepted'. Heavily patterned carpets in dark green, red or pink and white were the norm, with large, three–dimensional designs of flowers, animals, scrollwork and geometric motifs.

Except in dining rooms, floors were rarely fitted with wall–to–wall carpeting. Instead, a two–foot–wide margin around the perimeter of the room was left, with the floorboards then being stained, marbled, painted, stencilled, or filled with patterned parquetry. By the mid–1870s, fitted carpets began to disappear and were replaced by stained oak floorboards or parquet flooring, covered with a variety of exotic rugs, newly imported from Turkey, India and Persia. Hand–woven and animal–skin rugs were also in vogue. Those carpets that were being manufactured either imitated Oriental carpets or were designed by some of the leading artists of the day, including Morris and Voysey. As well as mass producing his stylized designs in a number of different weaves, Morris also became famous for his Hammersmith carpets, which were hand–knotted and inspired by ancient Oriental designs. However, because of their expense, these individually commissioned carpets and rugs were only available to the wealthy.

Parquet floors – waxed strips of contrasting coloured hardwoods with different patterned borders - were available in a wide variety of designs from the 1870s. Oriental rugs would then be scattered on top.

Carpets, however, were still expensive and were usually to be found only in the main reception rooms. Instead, cheaper alternatives were used in the rest of the house. The most popular was oilcloth, a painted and varnished canvas, which was hard–wearing, easy to keep clean, and most often fitted in hallways and bedrooms. Normally in sombre shades of brown or green, it was manufactured in a number of patterns, including imitation tiles and wood, Oriental designs and classical motifs. Plain oilcloths could also be stencilled.

Drugget, an inexpensive, coarse cloth, was another type of flooring used in the reception rooms. It most frequently served as a protective covering over good quality carpets, especially in dining rooms, but it was also laid on its own. Available with a patterned border, it could also be placed under a main rug or carpet to provide a decorative feature.

Linoleum was a Victorian invention, which from the mid–1870s found its way into halls, kitchens and bathrooms because of its durability and easy maintenance. It came in a number of finishes, including imitation wood, ceramic tiles, geometric patterns, and even William Morris floral designs.

Plain wooden floors also appeared, which could be stained, sanded (particularly in bedrooms), stencilled with floral or geometric designs, or painted to resemble other exotic woods or marble. The floorboards would then be covered with richly coloured and patterned rugs. Sometimes the wood was painted to simulate a carpet, with a single colour in the centre of the room and an elaborate border. In later Victorian times, lightly stained and polished oak was common as was parquet flooring. This look could also be achieved by staining planks of less expensive softwood.

Stone or slate floors, as well as quarry tiles, were used as flooring in halls and kitchen areas, but by the middle of the century encaustic tiles also came into widespread use.

The floors of the main
reception rooms in a Victorian
house were laid with deeply
patterned carpets or large
rugs in strong, warm colours.
The fashion prevailed for most
of the Victorian era. *Cohen &
Pearce. Osborne & Little plc*

Interior Details

The decorative details which completed the Victorian home not only echoed the battle of styles which prevailed throughout the nineteenth century, but also reflected the technological advances made during Victoria's reign. Revolutionary inventions and industrial developments meant that new methods of lighting, heating and tile production soon found their way into domestic buildings. With commercially manufactured goods becoming more rapidly available, and therefore increasingly less expensive, these new products were quickly within the reach of middle−class incomes. Most of these interior details are still to be found easily in antique and junk shops, whilst many original designs are now being copied and manufactured today.

Fireplaces

Each room in a Victorian house had a fireplace in it, which not only provided heat but also formed the focal point of the room. Therefore, as H.W. and A. Arrowsmith wrote in their *House Decorator's and Painter's Guide* in 1840, 'too much labour cannot be bestowed on the decoration of the chimneypiece, as it is the part of the room to which the attention is chiefly drawn'.

A range of mid–to–late Victorian cast–iron register grates and chimneypieces.

Classically inspired chimneypieces, wooden overmantels and simple mantelpieces were covered with statues, china and other ornaments so beloved by the Victorians. Patterned tiles were then inset into the sides. **Left:** *Stovax* 'Classic Fireplace' – Victorian tiled insert fireplace and pine Georgian mantel.
Below left: In the 1880s cast–iron houses and stoves were exported to Australia during the Gold Rush. This surviving example has planks from the packing cases lining its walls.

In the eighteenth and early nineteenth centuries, the most common form of fireplace was the hob grate, which had three or four bars across the front to hold in the coal, and two iron plates on either side on which kettles and saucepans were heated. These were manufactured by many companies, including Carron Company, for whom James Adam had designed hob grates with neo–classical decoration, and the Coalbrookdale Company, which pioneered new, cast–iron processing methods at its foundry. However, the hob grate was more efficient when burning wood than the newly available cheap coal, and by the 1840s the register grate had been developed which overcame the problems of draughts and the emission of sulphurous fumes. These grates had a metal plate across the chimney, which regulated the amount of smoke and created a smaller draught.

Early Victorian fire surrounds were simple and classical in design, with elegant pilasters and brackets. Made predominantly of marble, they would be of pure white or dove grey in the drawing room and of black or black and yellow in the dining room. Carved stone or wood were alternative materials used. In the bedrooms, fireplaces were smaller than in the reception rooms and were usually of painted wood.

As with everything else, as the century progressed fireplace designs became heavier and more ornate. Cast–iron grates became more common and by the 1850s new, semi–circular shapes vied in popularity with the traditional rectangular opening. Heavily decorated cast–iron mantelpieces, on intricately carved brackets, also began to be mass produced in the late 1850s. Patterned tiles in bold geometric or floral designs were then inset in their sides.

By the 1860s mantelpieces began to be swathed in material to match the lavish furnishings in the rest of the room. Velvet, lace and silk–covered pelmets, trimmed with fringes and frills, embellished the fireplace, with every kind of ornament displayed on top. However these draped mantelpieces fell out of fashion towards the end of the century.

Fire accessories were manufactured to complement the different styles of fireplace they served.

The fireplaces illustrated **right**, **below** and **opposite left** were designed by Philip Webb for Standen House, Sussex in 1894. Now owned by the National Trust, it is the only one of his houses to have survived and is a fine example of the architecture and interior decoration adopted by William Morris and his followers. **Below right:** An 1880s chimney piece made entirely of cast iron at Como House, Melbourne, Australia.

Above: The High Victorians covered every surface with frills and flounces, including the tops of mantelpieces.

Decorative cast–iron stoves were more common in Europe and America than in England These different styles appeared in a New York manufacturer's catalogue for 1898.

In reaction to these over–decorated looks, Arts and Crafts fireplaces resembled medieval styles, with simple wood or red brick chimneypieces and large free–standing grates. Inglenook fireplaces with copper smoke hoods were also revived. Otherwise, fireplaces were smaller, with a rectangular opening and a simple painted wooden frame inset with plain tiles.

By the end of the century, the sinuous forms of the Art Nouveau movement were well suited to all aspects of fireplace design.

Ironwork, brass and copper fire accessories sat beside the fireplace adding to its overall decoration, with gleaming fenders, andirons, fire–backs, coal skuttles, bellows, fire–irons, fire–baskets and fire–dogs manu–factured in the different styles prevalent throughout the century. Needlepoint firescreens embroidered by the women of the household completed the scene.

In Europe and America, wood– and coal–burning cast–iron stoves were a popular alternative type of heating in most rooms of the house, although in England they were usually only placed in hallways. Again, styles of stove and their decorative forms echoed the style of the rest of the house.

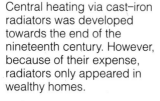

Central heating via cast–iron radiators was developed towards the end of the nineteenth century. However, because of their expense, radiators only appeared in wealthy homes.

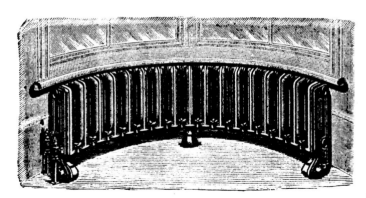

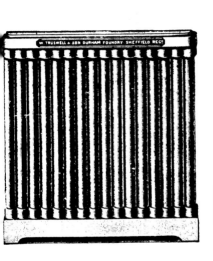

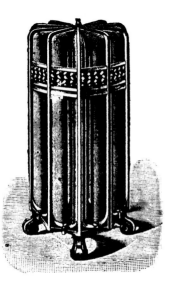

Lighting

The years 1820 to 1900 saw major changes in domestic lighting with the developments of paraffin and oil lamps, and of gas and electricity. As these new forms of lighting began to replace candles during the century, rooms became better lit, which had an enormous effect of interior decoration. The rich, dark colours of the High Victorian era only began to be adopted when internal lighting improved, although it was still dim by today's standards.

The paraffin lamp was introduced in 1845, but it was the invention of domestic gas lighting that had the most profound effect on Victorian homes. At first light fittings, connected to a gas pipe, had to be fixed to the walls and ceilings, with the result that candles, paraffin and oil lamps were still in use elsewhere in the room. However, by the 1850s table lamps were available that had a long rubber tube attached to the pipe, which enabled the lamp to be more mobile. The use of gas for internal lighting became more widespread in the late 1880s, after Carl Auer von Welsbach developed a mantle which became incandescent when heated over a gas flame, thus producing a brighter light. Another invention, the inverted mantle, which projected light downwards, also improved the amount of light obtained in a room.

Oil and gas hanging lights, wall brackets and table lamps provided the dim Victorian house with a modicum of light. When electricity introduced brighter light into the home in the 1880s, coloured glass,in the style of Louis Comfort Tiffany, and hand - painted porcelain shades became popular to soften the glare. These traditional Victorian designs are still being reproduced today.

In earlier centuries crystal chandeliers lit by candles had been a popular feature of formal reception rooms, a fashion which continued in the nineteenth century but with oil wicks or gas instead. These chandeliers and gasoliers were either of crystal or of metalwork, with highly ornate designs, and could be raised or lowered by a system of pulleys. Simpler hanging lamps were used in the less formal rooms, including the library and the kitchen. These had a vertical brass or iron bar which supported a horizontal bar, sometimes in the shape of a scroll. Along this were two or three lamps, with decorative opaque glass shades on them.

Wall brackets and sconces, fuelled by either oil or gas, were another common sight. Their supports were moulded into the shape of scrolls, leaves and flowers, and had glass shades in a variety of styles. Lily and tulip shapes were popular, as were plain–coloured, etched–glass shades, with fluted rims in a contrasting colour.

Tall parlour oil lamps were a popular form of lighting, with painted globe– and vase–shaped shades. As glass painting was a Victorian hobby, many of their floral designs and pictures were done by the women of the household. Student lamps, whose shades were supported by a vertical brass tube on a heavy brass base, made their appearance in libraries and studies.

In High Victorian times, lampshades were as overdressed as other objects in the room. Made of fabrics such as parchment, linen and silk, they were edged with elaborate frills, fringes and beadwork.

Most Victorian rooms had hanging lamps in the centre of their ceiling, which ranged from ornate metal and glass chandeliers in the main reception rooms to more simple styles in the kitchen and hallway.

Electricity was first introduced into the home in the 1880s, although, because of its expense and initial inefficiency, it was not in common usage until the turn of the century. However, the advent of electricity had a radical effect on lighting styles. Although still dim due to the low wattage of the first light bulbs, electric light was considerably brighter than any previous means of illumination. As a result, coloured or stained–glass shades were designed to diffuse the glare from this new, harsher light.

The man who most influenced the design of stained–glass lamps was Louis Comfort Tiffany. Fascinated by the glass mosaics of the Middle East, he created magnificent, brightly coloured, stained–glass lampshades, usually of flowers and fruit, set in intricately patterned cames. These leaded glass shades not only transformed the brighter light produced by electricity into a warm glow, but also provided a beautiful decorative object in itself. Imitation Tiffany lamps were soon commercially available, as they still are today.

In the 1890s, the Arts and Crafts movement also adopted simpler light fittings in wood– or metal–shaped frames. Inset in these were either patterned stained glass or plain glass etched with simple geometric or floral motifs. One of the main designers was W.A.S. Benson, who produced metal shades that deflected the light down wards, which softened the electric light.

In practice, however, Victorian homes were usually lit by a combination of all these kinds of lights, with candles in elaborate candle–holders still in use in dining rooms so as to create a more intimate atmosphere.

Late Victorian light fittings were enhanced by intricately moulded brass and sinuously curved and sculptured Art Nouveau metalwork.

Over-dressed fabric lampshades with patterned beading and fringes were a traditional feature of High Victorian style. It was not until later in the century that more delicate glass shades began to appear. However some oil lamps on bases shaped like classical urns and columns had plainer glass bowls.

Tiles

As we have already noted, tiles were a major decorative as well as practical feature of Victorian homes. They were hard–wearing, easy to keep clean, and available in a wide variety of patterns to enliven the floors and walls of both paths and entrance porches as well as of hallways, vestibules, kitchens and bathrooms; they were also used to decorate fireplaces, stoves, washstands and other pieces of furniture.

Although a traditional craft, the use of tiles for domestic flooring was revived in 1840 when Herbert Minton developed the encaustic tile, a method of inlaying different coloured clays and fusing them together during firing. Soon these tiles were being commercially manufactured by the numerous factories that sprang up to meet the new demand for them. Widely used by the Gothic Revivalists, who advocated fleur–de–lys and trefoil patterns, many geometric mosaics were also produced in the natural colours of the clay – white, black, red and cream being the normal hues, with blue, green and lilac becoming available later through the use of chemical dyes.

By the late 1870s, Charles Eastlake was enthusing that 'This branch of art–manufacture [encaustic tiles] is one of the most hopeful, in regard to taste, now carried on in this country. It has not only reached great technical perfection as far as material and colour are concerned, but, aided by the designs supplied by many architects of acknowledged skill, it has gradually become a means of decoration which, for beauty of effect, durability, and cheapness, has scarcely a parallel.' He went on to recommend that those of Messrs Maw & Co. of Salop

Art Nouveau motifs (**left**) and William Morris floral patterns (**below**) looked particularly effective on ceramic tilework.

Flowers, foliage and birds were popular subjects on Victorian decorative tiles. **Left:** *Original Style* Victorian picture tiles. **Below:** *Original Style* 'Birds and Butterfly'.

'stand almost unrivalled', although firms like Doulton and Minton were major producers. He also thought that 'an inlay of encaustic tiles, to a height, say, of three or four feet from the ground, would form an excellent lining for a hall or ground–floor passage'.

William Morris and his revival of traditional crafts greatly influenced the development of glazed wall tiles. His naturalistic and heraldic patterns soon embellished many a home, although it was one of his associates, William de Morgan, who was more influential in the field of ceramic design. Inspired by the beauty and colours of Islamic ornamentation, de Morgan used vivid colours, especially peacock blues and greens, and Turkish and Persian motifs. He also decorated tiles with a range of mythical animals, like the sea–dragon, as well as using realistic subjects like ships, birds and flowers. His hand–painted designs were too expensive for most people, but imitations soon appeared on the numerous tiles that began to be mass produced from the 1870s onwards.

Art Nouveau forms were especially suitable for tilework as their undulating patterns worked well in ceramicware. Usually in dark greens and browns, their floral motifs and lustrous glazes adorned many a porch, hallway and fireplace.

The art of painting tiles was also popular and provided women with an additional creative area to indulge in.

A range of elaborate encaustic tile patterns to be found in the halls of wealthier households.

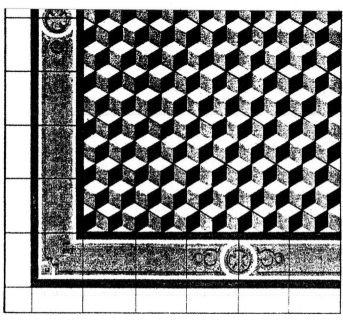

Chapter 6
The Victorian Garden

'Heated to a pleasant temperature, full of bright and
rare blooms the gentle breath of sweet–scented gardenias and tuberoses
pervades the atmosphere. Cages of many–coloured foreign birds, a gleam
of Moorish lamps against the greenery overhead, comfortable lounges,
wickerwork tables, Turkish rugs strewn on
the tesselated floor – all combine to make a delightful place in which to
while away Time with books or work.'

Mrs Alexander Fraser, novelist and hostess, describing her Sussex conservatory, c.1880

The conservatory was an ideal Victorian innovation, which combined new technological developments in ironwork and glazing with the nineteenth – century love of scientific and botanical exploration. *Town & Country Conservatories*

The Victorians were obsessed with Nature and filled their homes and gardens with dense greenery and exotic plants. New kinds of plants were constantly being discovered from all over the world by travellers and horticulturalists and brought to England for scientific study at the Royal Botanic Gardens at Kew; as a result, a vast range of exotic plants became known in England for the first time. This coincided with the development and manufacture of cheaper panes of glass and of ironwork, which led to the construction of vast conservatories like the Palm House at Kew in which these new, delicate plants could be housed and nurtured.

The rise of the middle classes who now possessed gardens of their own also added to the interest in rare plants and in garden landscaping. Unlike the aristocracy, who had teams of gardeners to tend their large estates, and the poor in rural areas who grew food for subsistence, the middle classes saw their gardens as another area in which to display their passion for decoration as they did not need to grow food in them because of the new availability of fresh fruit and vegetables in the suburbs due to the expansion of the railway networks. Gardening soon came to be seen as a perfectly respectable occupation for ladies to undertake – although most middle–class homes had a gardener as well – and a number of books and periodicals were launched to provide them with practical advice on all aspects of garden care, beginning with John Loudon's *The Encyclopaedia of Gardening* (1826) and *The Gardeners' Magazine*, which he founded in 1826. Loudon's influence soon spread across the Atlantic and in 1841 Andrew Jackson Downing published his *A Treatise on the Theory and Practice of Landscape*.

Conservatories

Orangeries and greenhouses had been in existence for several centuries, but a number of factors combined to make the conservatory, attached to the rear of a house, a mid–Victorian innovation. As we have mentioned, the introduction of tropical plants from all over the world, the reduction in the cost of glass, the greater availability of cheaper ironwork and new techniques in heating all made it possible for the Victorians to create a luxurious garden room in which to sit and to display the new exotic plants now in vogue.

A number of large glass structures had been built in the early Victorian era, but the most spectacular were those constructed by Joseph Paxton, originally the head gardener at Chatsworth. His conservatory there was used as the model for the Crystal Palace, a magnificent building which he designed for the Great Exhibition in 1851, using a ridge–and–furrow system of glazing supported by cast–iron columns, wrought–iron girders and timber. Originally sited in London's Hyde Park, the building was later taken down and re–erected at Sydenham in south London, where it remained until it was destroyed by fire in 1936.

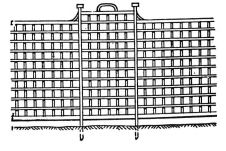

Soon even quite modest homes were attaching conservatories to them, if only a simple lean–to. It was also fashionable to have a conservatory leading off from the first–floor drawing room, so that guests could glimpse the lavish greenery through the doorway.

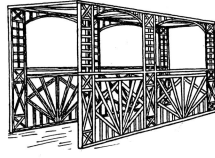

As Mrs Fraser describes, conservatories were also regarded as an extra room to relax in. As well as being filled with plants, they also contained cast–iron or wicker settees, chairs and tables, caged songbirds, fountains, statues, urns and rock gardens. Further decoration was added with patterned tiled floors covered with rugs, ornate iron details and stained– or etched–glass panes.

Gardens

The Victorian middle classes, with their small patches of garden, took to gardening with a passion, aided by the numerous manuals being published proffering tips of all kinds. As in everything else, the styles adopted by the aristocracy were imitated by the new monied class, although grand schemes were unsuitable for the small, rectangular gardens provided with the majority of terraced houses.

The Italian style of garden was the most popular until the 1870s, with its formal layout and symmetrical plan. From the house, a balustraded terrace with stone steps led down on to either a gravel path or the less common lawn. Along the edge were shrubberies filled with evergreens and geometrically shaped flower–beds, which usually contained

The formal Italian garden (**bottom right**) which was popular throughout the first half of Victoria's reign, was replaced in the 1870s by the desire to return to a more natural look. However, in the 1890s garden designers reintroduced a degree of formality by the use of such features as trellised walkways.

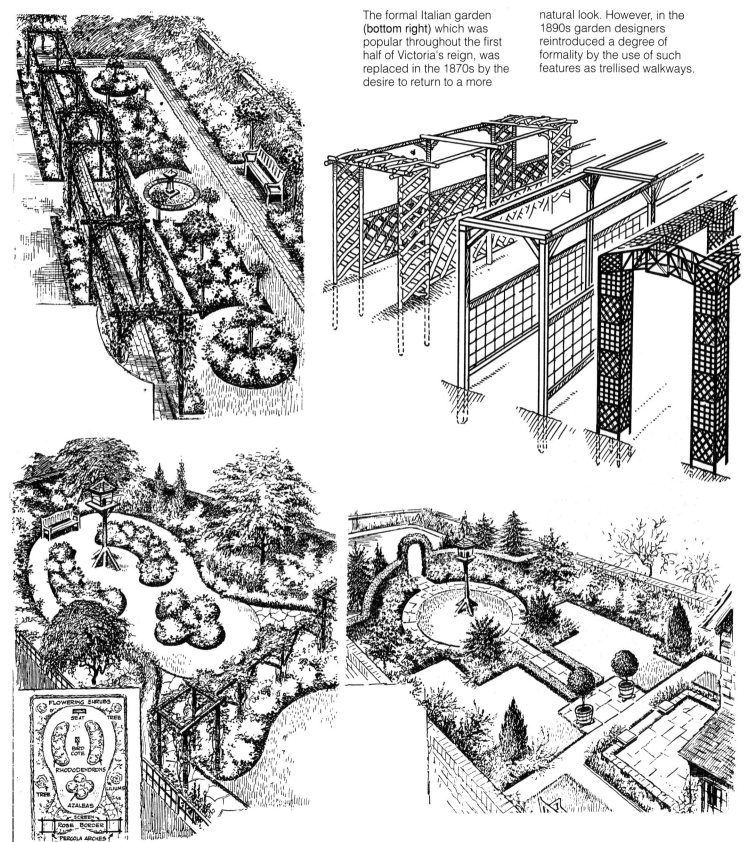

FLOWERING SHRUBS
SEAT   TREE
BIRD COTE.
RHODODENDRONS
LILIUMS
TREE
AZALEAS
SCREEN
ROSE BORDER
PERGOLA ARCHES

either one kind of plant or one overall colour scheme; these then had ornamental iron or terracotta borders. In the centre was a classical fountain, with statues, plant–filled urns and a sundial placed strategically around the garden.

However, by the 1870s the Arts and Crafts movement, inspired by the traditional country cottage garden, was advocating the return of the natural garden. The most important garden writer of this time was William Robinson, who started *The Garden* in 1871. Robinson abhorred the formal garden and called for the creation of a garden layout that showed plants in their natural state: the garden 'should rise out of its site and conditions as happily as a primrose out of a cool bank', he wrote. Wide lawns, herbaceous borders, and informal beds full of wild flowers were features of his gardens, as were rustic paths of gravel, stone or grass.

Gertrude Jekyll, the famous garden designer who collaborated with Edwin Lutyens from the 1890s, was greatly influenced by Robinson's work. She merged the natural school of garden design with the new architectural style advocated by the Queen Anne Revivalist, John Sedding, who reintroduced formality into the garden through the use of architectural details such as topiaries and trellised walks. Jekyll succeeded in balancing natural planting with a more formal landscape, in order to achieve what to her was the main purpose of a garden: 'to give delight and to give refreshment of mind, to soothe, to refine and to lift up the heart'.

Garden Furniture

Until the last quarter of the nineteenth century, gardens were furnished as extravagantly as inside the home. Ornate cast–iron benches, chairs and tables were manufactured in naturalistic shapes, including inter–woven branches, ferns, vines and plants. Snakes were also to be found curling around chair and table legs, as were rococo curlicues and scrolls which adorned more classically inspired shapes. Greek and Roman stone statues, flower urns on pedestals, fountains, sundials, iron or wood trellis–work on walls and arches, and elaborate cast–iron or terracotta flower–bed borders were features of most High Victorian gardens.

Styles eventually became simpler later in the century, with plain oak or elm benches, terracotta flowerpots, low stone troughs and stone sundials being found in the more informal, natural gardens inspired by the Arts and Crafts designers.

Opposite: The Victorians placed their conservatories so that their exotic plants and classical decor could be admired by guests in the main drawing room. **This page:** An authentic conservatory can be restored or added on to any Victorian home today because many of the original designs are being reproduced once more. *Town & Country Conservatories*

Stockists

The lists of suppliers given on these pages cannot be exhaustive and are intended only as a starting point. Local papers and commercial telephone directories are always worth looking at and are good sources of information about your own area. Alternatively there are many organisations giving specialist information and advice and those who will search for specific items.

UNITED KINGDOM

Information & Advice

Architectural Antique
Search
Cliffe Cottages
Parsons Green
Wetherby
West Yorks LS22 4RF
Will buy or locate architectural salvage piece required by client.

Architectural Salvage
Netley House
Gomshall
Surrey GU5 2QA
Index of architectural items. For a fee of £10 they will put buyers in touch with sellers. They do not keep items for sale.

British Decorators Association
6 Haywra Street
Harrogate
North Yorkshire HG1 5BL
Over 1,000 members who specialise in the decoration of period homes.

The Brooking Collection
Woodhay
White Lane
Guildford
Surrey GU4 8PU
Unique record of the development of period detail. Information and advice available.

Redundant Church
  Furnishings
Church Commissioners
1 Millbank
London SW1P 3JZ
Will supply contents register listing items from redundant churches.

The Victorian Society
1 Priory Gardens
Bedford Park,
London W4 1TT
Advice on restoration and preservation of Victorian buildings.

Architectural Antiques & Salvage

Ace Demolition & Salvage
Barrack Road
West Parley
Nr Hurn
Wimborne
Dorset

Alexander the Grate
126-128 Donegal Pass
Belfast B17 1BZ

Andy Thornton
Architectural Antiques
Ainleys Industrial Estate
Elland
West Yorks HXS 9JP

An Englishman's Home
56 Stokes Croft
Bristol
Avon BS1 3QU

Architectural Heritage
of Leicester
107-109 Highcross Street
Leicester LE1 4PH

Baileys Architectural
Antiques
The Engine Shed
Ashburton Industrial Estate
Ross-on-Wye
Herefordshire HR9 7BW

Barewood Trading Company
32-36 Kent Street
Smithfield
Belfast B11 2JA

Beacon Architectural
Salvage
The Old School
Alderminster
Stratford upon Avon
Warwickshire CV37 8NY

Bridgewater Reclamation Ltd
Old Co-op Dairy
Monmouth Street
Bridgewater
Somerset TA6 5EH

Brighton Architectural
Salvage
33 Gloucester Road
Brighton
Sussex BN1 4AQ

Britannia Restorations
Old Britannia House
Castle Street
Coombe Martin
nr Ilfracombe
North Devon EX34 0JF

Burtonhill Demolition Ltd
Vuncanworks
Floors Street
Johnstone
Renfrewshire PA5 8QS

Bygones Building Supplies
Broadlands
Whitstable Road
Blean
nr Canterbury
Kent CT2 9JQ

Cantabrian Antiques &
Architectural Salvage
16 Park Street
Lynton
North Devon

Churchill's Architectural
Salvage
212 Old Kent Road
London SE1 5TY

City Salvage
Ferry Road
Grangetown
Cardiff CF1 7JL

Conservation Building
Products Ltd
Forge Works
Forge Lane
Cradley Heath
Warley
West Midlands B64 5AL

Counterparts Demolition Ltd
Station Road
Topsham
Exeter
Devon EX3 0EF

T Crowther & Son Ltd
282 North End Road
Fulham
London SW6 1NH

Cumbria Architectural
Salvage
Birks Hill
Raughton Head
Carlisle
Cumbria CA5 7DH

Dorset Restoration
Cow Drove
Bere Regis
Wareham
Dorset BH20 7JZ

Edinburgh Architectural
Salvage Yard (EASY)
Unit 6
Couper Street
off Coburg Street
Leith
Edinburgh EH6 6HH

Fens Restoration
46 Lots Road
Chelsea
London SW10 0QF

Frederick's Ltd
Frederick's Barn
rear of 24 London Road
Southborough
Kent TN4 0QB

The Furniture Cave
533 King's Road
London SW10 0TZ

Ed Glover
The Oasthouse
Wyckl Lane
East Worldham
nr Alton
Hants GU34 3AW

Glover & Stacey Ltd
Grange Farm Buildings
Grange Road
Tongham
Farnham
Surrey GU10 1DN

Heritage Scotland Ltd
Heritage Centre
Lower Balman Street
Montrose
Angus DD10 8AZ

The House Hospital
68 Battersea High Street
London SW11 3HX

The House Hospital
Baldwins Farm
The Dymock Road
nr Newent
Glos GL18 1LS

Hallidays Antiques Ltd
The Old College
Dorchester-on-Thames
Oxon

Havenplan's Architectural
Emporium
The Old Station
Station Road
Killamarsh
Sheffield
South Yorks S31 8EN

In Situ
238 Seymour Grove
Old Trafford
Manchester M16 0LH

LASSco
St Michael's Church
Mark Street
Shoreditch
London EC2A 5ER

Maltings Demolition Sales
The Old Malt Kilns
Station Road
Barnby Don
Doncaster
South Yorks DN3 1HQ

Malton Reclamation & Sales
46 Hatchpond Road
Nuffield Industrial Estate
Poole
Dorset DH17 7JZ

North West Architectural
Antiques
Old Colliery Buildings
Burtonhead Road
Ravenhead
St Helens
Merseyside WA9 5DX

Oxford Architectural Antiques
The Old Depot
Belson Street
Jericho
Oxford OX2 6BE

Posterity Architectural
Effects
Baldwins Farm
Dynmock Road
Newent
Glos GL18 1LS

The Pumping Station
Penarth Road
Cardiff
South Glam CF1 7TT

A L Rattry
Craighall Rattray
Blairgowrie
Perthshire PH10 7JB

Reclaimed Materials
Northgate
White Land Industrial
Estate
Morecambe
Lancs LA3 3AY

R & R Reclamation
Top Farm
Kirton Road
Blyton
nr Gainsborough
Lincs DN21 3PE

The Reclamation Trading Co
22 Elliot Road
Love Lane Industrial Estate
Cirencester
Glos GL7 1YG

Romsey Reclamation
Station Approach
Railway Station
Romsey
Hants SO51 8DU

Seymours Architectural
Salvage
17 Beck Street
Portsea
Portsmouth
Hants PO1 3AN

Sherwood Architectural
  Salvage
73-77 Victoria Road
Sherwood
Nottingham NG5 2NE

Solopark Ltd
The Old Railway Station
Station Road
nr Pampisford
Cambs CB2 4HB

Southern Architectural
Salvage
Oaktree Rarm
Bashley Cross Road
Bashley
New Milton
Hants BH25 5SY

Southern Demolition (Poole)
24 Gough Crescent
Poole
Dorset DH17 7JQ

Townsends (London) Ltd
1 Church Street
London NW8 8EE
and also at
36 New End Square
London NW3

Walcot Reclamation
108 Walcot Street
Bath
Avon BA1 5BG

Wells Reclamation Company
The Old Cider Farm
Wells Road
Coxley nr Wells
Somerset BA5 1RQ

Wilson Reclamation Services
Yewtree Barn
Newton-in-Lartmel
nr Grange-over-Sands
Cumbria CA11 6JU

Mouldings

ABC Studios (Mouldings) Ltd
Oxford Lane
City Road
Cardiff CF2 3DU

Alderage Timber Products
Old Park Farm Yard
Main Road
Kingsley
Hants GU32 9LU

Alexander Ltd
Unit 2B
Birch Close
Eastbourne
East Sussex BN23 6PE

Allied Guilds
Unit 19
Reddicap Trading Estate
Coleshill Road
Sutton Coalfield
West Midlands B75 7BU

Architectural Castings
59 The Arches
New Kings Road
Putney
London SW6 4PR

Architectural & Industrial GRP
562 Kingston Road
Raynes Park
London SW20 8DR

Architectural Mouldings Ltd
City Business Centre
Hemmingsdale Road
Gloucester
Glos GL2 6HN

Aristocast Originals
Bold Street
Sheffield S9 2LR

Arkwright Decorative
Plastering
Unit 3 New Road
Hounslow
Middx TW3 2AN

Artistic Plastercraft
Lyndhurst Studios
16-18 Lyndhurst Road
Bath
Avon BA2 3JH

H & F Badcock
(Fibrous & Solid
Plastering) Ltd
Unit 9
57 Sandgate Road
Old Kent Road
Peckham
London SE15 1LE

Bangor Plaster Mouldings
18A Groomsport Road
Bangor
Co Down BT20 5AZ

Copley Decor Mouldings
Bedale Road
Leyburn
North Yorks DL8 5QA

Craigavon Cornicing
Site 11
Ulster Street Industrial
Area
Ulster Street
Lurgan BT67 9RN

F H Crocker
Corzier Road
Mutley
Plymouth
Devon PL4 7LN

W G Crotch
10 Tuddenham Avenue
Ipswich
Suffolk IP4 2HE

Decorative Plasterwork
385 Ladbroke Grove
London W10 5AA

Delmar R M C Ltd
Manor Royal
Crawley
Surrey RH10 2XQ

Eaten-Gaze Ltd
86 Teesdale Street
London E2

Editha Plasterers
63 Peabody Hill
West Dulwich
London SE21

Fine Art Associates
Unit 2 Heath Works
Grove Road
Chadwell Heath
Essex RM6 4UR

G C Mouldings
10 West End Lane
Barnet
Herts EN5 2SA

L Grandison & Son
Innerleithen Road
Peebles
Tweeddale EH45 8BA

Hallidays
The Old College
Dorchester-on-Thames
Oxon OX9 8HL

E J Harmer & Co Ltd
19A Birkbeck Hill
London SE21 8JS

Locker & Riley Ltd
Capital House
Bruce Groce
Wickford
Essex SS11 8DB

London Fine Art Plaster
7-9 Audrey Street
London E2 8QH

Malvern Studios
56 Cowleigh Road
Malvern
Worcs WR14 1QD

Mid Antrim Plaster
Mouldings
34 Church Street
Andgill
Ballymena

E G Millar (Plastering) Ltd
54 Hawkwood Crescent
Chingford
London E4 7PJ

K & H M Moyle
(Ornamental Plasterers)
Unit 9
Old Mills Industrial Estate
Paulton
nr Bristol BS18 5SU

Nicholl Plaster Mouldings
81 Knockbracken Road
Castlereach BT6 9SP

Picasso Classic Mouldings
34 Locarno Road
Moorends
Doncaster
South Yorks

The Plaster Decoration Co Ltd
30 Stannary Street
London SE11 4AE

Potter's of Houghton
The Wheelwrights
Houghton
Stockbridge
Hants SO20 6LW

Regency Moulding
Unit 1E
Yeo Road
Colley Lane Industrial
Estate
Bridgwater
Somerset TA6 5HG

Riverside Mouldings
Unit 18
Riverside Industrial Estate
Riverway
London SE10 0BH

George Rome (Ornamental
Plasterwork) Ltd
33 Townsend Street
Glasgow G4 0LA

Sandhurst Stone Mouldings
Unit 1
rear of Wellington Road
Sandhurst
Surrey GU17 8AW

Jane Schofield
50 Fore Street
Bradninch
Devon EX5 4NN

M E Short
Hewitts Estate
Elmbridge Road
Cranmleigh
Surrey GU6 8LW

Simply Elegant
Callywhite Lane
Dronfield
Sheffield
South Yorks S18 0XP

Solway Studios
(Ornamental Plasterers)
76 High Street
Kircudbright DG6 4JL

Stevensons of Norwich Ltd
Roundtree Way
Norwich
Norfolk NR& 8SH

T & O Plaster Casting
7 Collier Row
Romford
Essex RM95 3NP

Tiles

A G Tiles
Dividy Road
Bucknall
Stoke-on-Trent
Staffs ST2 0JB

Sally Anderson Tiles
Parndon Mill
Harlow
Essex CM20 2HP

Bernard J Arnull & Co
12-14 Queen Street
London W1

The Art Tile Company Ltd
Etruria Tile Works
Garner Street
Etruria, Stoke-on-Trent

Fired Earth
Middle Aston
Oxfordshire OX5 3PX

Flooring Supplies Ltd
Bernard Works
Bernard Road
London N15 4NE

Hereford Tiles Ltd
Whitestone
Hereford HR1 3SF

H & R Johnson Tiles Ltd
Highgate Tile Works
Tunstall, Stoke-on-Trent

Maw & Co Ltd
342 High Street
Tunstall
Stoke-on-Trent

Original Style
Falcon Road
Sowton Industrial Estate
Exeter EX2 7LF

Paris Ceramics
543 Battersea Park Road
London SW11 3BL

Dennis Ruabon Ltd
Haford Tileries
Ruabon
Wrexham, Clwyd

Fireplaces

Acquisitions Fireplaces Ltd
269 Camden High Street
London NW1 7BX

Aga Rayburn
PO Box 30 Ketley
Telford, Shropshire

Amazing Grates
Phoenix House
61-63 High Road
East Finchley
London N2 8AB

Anglia Fireplaces
Kendal House
1 Cambridge Road
Impington

By The Fire
Thames Street
Wallingford
Oxford

Cantabrian Antiques
Park Street
Lynton
Devon

The Cast Iron Fireplace Co
Ltd
103 East Hill
Wandsworth
London SW18

Design Fireplaces
Walnut Tree Close
Guildford

Dovre Castings
Unit 81
Castle Vale Industrial Estate
Minworth
Sutton Coldfield B76 8AL

Feature Interiors
34 Seymour Road
Bournemouth
Dorset

The Firesurround Centre
Worsley Mill
Manchester 1

Flames & Coal
147 Kings Road
Brentwood

Franco-Belge
Unit 81
Castle Vale Industrial Estate
Minworth
Sutton Coldfield B76 8AL

Robin Gage
50 Pimlico Road
London SW1 W8LP

Gibson & Goold Ltd
3 Scotland Street
Glasgow G5 8LS

Grate Designs
49 Camden Road
Tunbridge Wells
Kent

Harrogate Fireplaces
38-40 Kings Road
North Yorkshire

Heatwave
117 St Johns Hill
Sevenoaks

Home Flame
Romiley Road
Canton, Cardiff

Ideal Fireplaces
300 Upper Richmond Road
West
East Sheen
London SW14 7JG

Ironmasters
148 Stockport Road
Cheedle

Marble Hill Fireplaces
72 Richmond Road
Twickenham
Middlesex

Morley Stove Shop
Coronation Hall
Coronation Road
Ware, Herts

The Original Choice
1340 Stratford Road
Hall Green
Birmingham B28 9EH

Stovax Ltd
Falcon Road
Sowton Industrial Estate
Exeter EX2 7LF

Phoenix
51 Lark Lane
Liverpool L17 8UW

Pope Fireplaces
Rear of 62-64 High Street
Barnet, Herts

Realistic Fires
135 Kingston Road
Wimbledon
London SW15

Mark Ripley Antiques & Forge
Robertsbridge, Sussex

The Sussex Fireplace Centre
Hill House
56 Western Road
Hove, Sussex

Thermocet UK
Real Fire Heating Centre
Telford Way
Kettering NN16 8UN

Woodford Fire of Weybridge
84 Church Street
Weybridge

Woods, Fireplace Design
160-162 Oak Street
St Martins Gate
Norwich NR3 3BU

Stained Glass

Acanthus
143 Northfields Avenue
London W13 9QR

Mark Angus
Church Road Studio
Combe Down
Bath
Avon

Bournemouth Stained Glass
Seamoor Lane
Westbourne
Bournemouth
Dorset BR4 9AU

Susan Bradbury
3 Orchard Studios
Brook Green
London W6

Susan M Cook
The Stained Glass Studio
Unit 117
31 Clerkenwell Close
London EC1R 0AT

Creative Glass
140d Redland Road
Bristol
Avon BS6 6YA

Daedalian Glass Ltd
Pontenoire House
286 Talbot Road
Blackpool FY1 3QS

Glasslight Studios
The Old Pumphouse
Gloucester Place
The Maritime Quarter
Swansea SA1 1TY

The Glass Market
Old Mill House
Temple
Marlow
Bucks SL7 1LA

Inside Art Ltd
1-3 Petersfield Road
Bordon
Hants

Lamplight Studio
10 Barley Mow Passage
Chiswick
London W4 4PH

Lead & Light
15 Camden Lock
Commercial Place
London NW1 8AF

Matthew Lloyd
Stained Glass Studios
63 Amberlety Road
Palmers Green
London N13 4BH

Long Eaton Stained Glass
1 Northcote Street
Long Eaton
Notts NG10 1EZ

Prisms Stained Glass Design
34 Boundary Road
London NW8 0HG

Paul Quail
Boundary Farmhouse
Swanton Road
Gunthorpe
Norfolk NR24 2NS

Sologlas Ltd
Sologlas Technical Advisory
Service
Herald Way
Binley Coventry CV3 2ND

Stained Glass Construction &
Design
62 Fairfield Street
London SW18 1DY

Sunrise Stained Glass
58/60 Middle Street
South Street
Hants PO5 4BP

Caroline Swash
88 Woodwarde Road
London SE22 8UT

Bathrooms

Many architectural salvage experts supply original bathrooms, but it is possible to buy good reproduction Victorian designs made using modern methods and easy to fit modern plumbing.

A Touch of Brass
123 Kensington Church St
London W8

W Adams & Son
Westfield Works
Spon Lane
West Bromwich
West Midlands
B70 6BH

Barber Wilsons & Co Ltd
Crawley Road
London N22 6AH

Adamsez Ltd
Dukesway
Team Valley
Gateshead
Tyne & Wear
NE1 0SW

Heritage Bathrooms
Taddington Manor
Taddington
Cutsdean
Cheltenham
Glos GL54 5RY

Hill House Interiors
Rotunda Buildings
Montpellier Circus
Cheltenham
Glos

Pipe Dreams
103-105 Regents Park Road
London NW1 8UR

B C Sanitan
Unit 12 Nimrod Way
Elgar Road
Reading
Berks RG2 0EB

The Traditional Bathroom
Warehouse
92 Carnwath Road
Fulham
London SW6

Victoriana Bathrooms Ltd
439 Cleethorpe Road
Grimsby
South Humberside
DN31 3BU

USA

Architectural Details & Salvage

1874 House
8070 SE 13th Avenue
Portland
Oregon 97202

ADI
2045 Broadway
Kansas City
Missouri 64108

Architectural Salvage
Cooperative
1328 East 12th Street
Davenport
Iowa 52803

Architectural Salvage
Warehouse
337 Berry Street
Brooklyn
New York
NY 11211

Florida Victorian
Architectural Antiques
901 W 1 St (W Hwy 46)
Sanford
Florida 32771

Great American Salvage
34 Cooper Square
New York
NY 10003

Housewreckers NB
& Salvage Co
396 Somerset Street
New Brunswick
New Jersey 08901

Kayne & Son
Custom Forged Hardware
76 Daniel Ridge Road
Candler
North Caroline 28715

New Boston Building
Wrecking Co Inc
84 Arsenal Street
Watertown
Massachusetts 02172

Ohmega Salvage
2406 San Pablo Avenue
Berkeley
California 94702

Off the Wall
Architectural Antiques
950 Glenneyre Street
Laguna Beach
California 92651

Old Home Building
& Restoration
PO Box 384
West Suffield
Connecticut 06093

Old House-New House
Restoration
169 N Victoria Street
St Paul
Minnesota 55104

Pagliacco Turning & Milling
PO Box 225
Woodacre
California 94973

Pasternak's Emporium
2515 Morse Street
Houston
Texas 77019

Price & Viser Millwork
2536 Valencia Street
Bellingham
Washington 98226

Red Baron's
6320 Roswell Road
Atlanta
Georgia 30328

Roland Millwork & Lumber
393 North Pearl Street
Albany
NY 12207

Salvage One
1524 S Sangamon Street
Chicago
Illinois 60608

Second Chance
230 7th Street
Macon
Georgia 31202

Shakertown Corporation
PO Box 400
Winlock
Washington 98596

Silver Creek Mill
Englers Block
1335 W Hwy 76
Branson
Missouri 65616

The Smoot Lumber Company
PO Box 26188
1201 N Royal Street
Alexandria
Virginia 22313

Speciality Building Supply
PO Box 13529
Jackson
Mississippi 39326

Strip Shop
2201 Tchoupitoulas Street
New Orleans
Louisiana 70130

United House Wrecking Corp
535 Hope Street
Stamford
Connecticut 06906

Urban Archaeology
137 Spring Street
New York
NY 10012

Victorian Warehouse
190 Grace Street
Auburn
California 95603

You Name It Inc
Box 1013
Middletown
Ohio 45044

Moldings - wood, plaster - door furniture

Acorn Manufacturing Co Inc
457 School Road
PO Box 31
Mansfield
Massachusetts 02048

Alexandria Wood Joinery
Plumer Hill Road
Alexandria
New Hampshire 03222

American Wood Column
Corporation
913 Grand Street
Brooklyn
New York
NY 11211

Anglo-American Brass
Company
PO Box 9487
San Jose
California 95157

Anthony Wood Products
PO Box 1081-S
Hilsboro
Texas 76645

Antique Hardware
509 Tangle Drive
Jamestown
North Carolina 27282

Archicast
1316 Madison
Memphis
Tennessee 38104

Architectural Stairbuilding &
Handrailing
62 Pioneer Street
Cooperstown
New York 13326

Ashwood Restoration
76 New Broadway
2nd Floor
North Tarrytown
New York 10591

Baldwin Hardware
Corporation
841 Wyoming Blvd
Box 15048
Reading
Pennsylvania 19612

Ball & Ball
463 W Lincoln Hwy
Exton
Pennsylvania 19341

Bare Wood Inc
106 Ferris Street
Brooklyn
NewYork
NY 11231

Beech River Mill Co
Old Rt 16
Centre Ossipee
New Hampshire 03814

Bona Decorative Hardware
3073 Madison Road
Cincinnati
Ohio 45209

Breakfast Woodworks
Louis Mackall PC
50 Maple Street
Branford
Connecticut 06405

Campbell, Marion
39 Wall Street
Bethlehem
Pennsylvania 18018

Carpenter & Smith
Restorations
Box 504
Highland Park
Illinois 60035

Customwood Manufacturing
  Company
PO Box 26208
Albuquerque
New Mexico 87125

David Woods Restoration
& Rehab Corp
129 Academy Street
Poughkeepsie
New York 12601

Decorative Hardware Studio
PO Box 627
180 Hunts Lane
Chappaqua
NY 10514

Decorators Supply Corp
3610-12 S Morgan St rear
Chicago
Illinois 60609

Dibbleville Door Works
504 Main Street
Fenton
Michigan 48430

Driwood Molding Company
PO Box 1729
Florence
South Carolina 29503

Drums Sash & Door Co Inc
PO Box 207
Drums
Pennsylvania 18222

Early New England
Rooms & Exteriors Inc
PO Box 377
East Windsor Hill
Connecticut 06028

Elephant Hill Iron Works
RR 1 Box 168
Tunbridge
Vermont 05077

Elk Valley Woodworking Inc
Rt 1 Box 88
Carter
Oklahoma 73627

Felber Studios Inc
110 Ardmore Ave
Box 551A
Ardmore
Pennsylvania 19003

C G Girolami & Sons
944 N Spaulding Avenue
Chicago
Illinois 60651

Hippo Hardware & Trading
Co
201 SE 12th Avenue
Portland
Oregon 97214

Hosek Manufacturing Co
4877 National Western Drive
205 Denver
Colorado 80216

International Building
Components
Box 51
Glenwood
NY 14069

Jeraud Paul Jordan Gallery
PO 71 Slade Acres
Ashford
Connecticut 06278

The Joinery Co
PO Box 518 OC8
Tarboro
North Carolina 27886

Kayne & Son
Custom Forged Hardware
76 Daniel Ridge Road
Candler
North Caroline 28715

Kenmore Industries
1 Thompson Square
PO Box 34
Boston
Massachusetts 02129

L H Freedman Studios
368 Congress St 5th Floor
Boston
Massachusetts 02210

Mad River Wood Works
PO Box 163
Arcata
California 95521

Mangione Plaster
21 John Street
Saugerties
NY 12477

Master Wood Carver
103 Corrine Drive
Pennington
New Jersey
Mr Trim
PO Box 1853
Louisville
Tennessee 37777

W F Norman Corporation
PO Box 323
Nevada
Missouri 64772

Old & Elegant Distributing
10203 Main Street Lane Dept
OHJ
Bellevue
Washington 98004

Oregan Wooden Screen
Door Co
330 High Street
Eugene
Oregon 97401

Ornamental Design Studios
1715 President Street
Brooklyn
NY 11213

Pagliacco Turning & Milling
PO Box 225
Woodacre
California 94973

Perkins Architectural
Millwork & Hardwood
Moldings
Rt 5 Box 264-W
Longview
Texas 75601

Pinecrest
2118 Blaisdell Avenue
Minneapolis
Minnesota 55404

Price & Viser Millwork
2536 Valencia Street
Bellingham
Washington 98226

Richmond Doors
PO Box 65
Manchester
New Hampshire 03105

Roland Millwork & Lumber
393 North Pearl Street
Albany
NY 12207

Second Chance
230 7th Street
Macon
Georgia 31202

Silver Creek Mill
Englers Block
1335 W Hwy 76
Branson
Missouri 65616

The Smoot Lumber Company
PO Box 26188
1201 N Royal Street
Alexandria
Virginia 22313

Speciality Building Supply
PO Box 13529
Jackson
Mississippi 39326

Van Dyke Supply Company
Box 278
Woonsocket
SD 57385

Walbrook Mill & Lumber
Co Inc
2636 W North Avenue
Baltimore
Maryland 21216

J P Weaver Co
2301 W Victory Blvd
Burbank
California 91506

Williamsburg Blacksmiths Inc
1 Buttonshop Road
Williamsburg
Massachusetts 01096

Windham Millworks
PO Box 1358
Windham
Maine 04062

World of Molding
3103 S Main Street
Santa Ana
California 92707

Sanitary Ware

A-Ball Plumbing Supply
1703 W Burnside Street
Portland
Oregon 97209

Antique Baths & Kitchens
2220 Carlton Way
Santa Barbara CA 93109

Baldwin Hardware
 Corporation
841 Wyoming Blvd
Box 15048
Reading
Pennsylvania 19612

Bona Decorative Hardware
3073 Madison Road
Cincinnati
Ohio 45209

Decorative Hardware Studio
PO Box 627
180 Hunts Lane
Chappaqua
NY 10514

Lena's Antique Bathroom
Fixtures
PO Box 1022
Bethel Island
California 94511

Mac the Antique Plumber
885 57th Street OC-87
Sacramento
California 95819

Old & Elegant Distributing
10203 Main Street Lane Dept
OHJ
Bellevue
Washington 98004

Omnia Industries Inc
Box 330
Cedar Grove
New Jersey 07009

The Sink Factory
2140 San Pablo Avenue
Berkeley
California 94702

Vintage Tub & Sink
 Restoration Service
701 Center Street
Ludlow
Massachusetts 01056

Lighting

B & P Lamp Supply Co Inc
Route 3
McMinnville
Tennessee 37110

Georgia Lighting
Supply Co Inc
530 14th Street NW
Atlanta
Georgia 30318

Illustrious Lighting
1925 Fillmore Street
San Francisco
California 94115

The Kardell Studio Inc
904 Westminster Street NW
Washington DC 20001

William Spencer Inc
Creek Road
Rancocas Woods
New Jersey 08060

Unique Art Glass Co Inc
5060 Arsenal
St Lousi
Missouri 63139

Yankee Craftsman
357 Commonwealth Road
Rt 30
Wayland
Massachusetts 01778

Glass

Backstrom Stained Glass
et al
PO Box 2311
Columbus
Mississippi 39704

Bygone Era Architectural
Antiques
4783 Peachtree Road
Atlanta
Georgia 30341

Canal Company
1612 14th Street NW
Washington DC 20009

The Cedar Guild
51579 Gates Bridge E
Gates
Oregon 97346

Curran Art Glass Inc
4520 Irving Park Road
Chicago
Illinois 60641

Glass Arts
30 Penniman Road
Boston
Massachusetts 02314

Golden Age Glassworks
Bellvale Road
Warwick
NY 10990

Great Gatsbys
5070 Peachtree Ind Blvd
Chamblee
Georgia 30341

Morgan Bockius Studios Inc
1412 York Road
Warminster
Pennsylvania 18974

Tiles, marble, stone

American Olean Tile Co
PO Box 271
Lansdale
Pennsylvania 19446

Designs in Tile
PO Box 4983 Dept C
Foster City
California 94404

Firebird Inc
335 Snyder Avenue
Berkeley Heights
New Jersey 07922

The New England Slate Co
Smid Incorporated
Sudbury
Vermont 05733

New York Marble Works Inc
1399 Park Avenue
New York
NY 10029

Penn Big Bed Slate Co Inc
PO Box 184
Slatington
Pennsylvania 18080

Roman Marble Co
120 W Kinzie
Chicago
Illinois 60610

Starbuck Goldner
315 W 4th Street
Bethlehem
Pennsylvania 18015

Terra Designs Inc
19 Market Street
Morristown
New Jersey 07960

United States Ceramic
Tile Company
10233 Sandyville Road SE
East Sparta
Ohio 44626

Helen Williams - Delft Tiles
12643 Hortense Street
Studio City
California 91604

Fireplaces

Barnstable Stove Shop
Box 472 Rt 149
Massachusetts 02668

Brick Stove Works
374 Nelson Ridge Road
Washington
Maine 04574

Bryant Stove Works
RFD 2 Box 2048
Thorndike
Maine 04986

C & D Distributors
Hearth Mate
PO Vox 766
Old Saybrook
Connecticute 06475

Homestead Chimney
PO Box 5182
Clinton
New Jersey 08809

Hearth Realities
PO Box 38903
Atlanta
Georgia 30334

The Reggio Register Co
]20 Central Avenue
PO Box 511
Ayer
Massachusetts 01432

Saltbox
3004 Columbia Avenue
Lancaster
Pennsylvania 17603

Vermont Castings Inc
Prince Street
Randolph
Vermont 05060

Woodstock Soapstone Co Inc
Airpark Road
Box 37H/395
W Lebanon
New Hampshire 03784

Worthington Hardware Co Inc
22 N Main Street
St Charles
Missouri 63301

Wall finishes

Bentley Brothers
918 Baxter Avenue
Louisville
Kentucky 40204

Bradbury & Bradbury
Wallpapers
PO Box 155-C
Benicia
California 94510

J R Burrows & Co
PO Box 418
Cathedral Station
Boston
Massachusetts 02118

Cyrus Clark Co Inc
267 Fifth Avenue
New York
NY 10016

Good & Co
Floor-cloth makers
Box 387-OHJ
Dublin
New Hampshire 03444

Hand-Stenciled Interiors
590 King Street
Hanover
Massachusetts 02339

Judith Hendershot & Assoc
1408 Main Street
Evanstown
Illinois 60202

Katzenbach & Warren Inc
23645 Mercantile Road
Cleveland
Ohio 44122

Mile Hi Crown Inc
1925 Blake St Suite 100
Denver
Colorado 80202

Prater-Northey
17159 Beaver Springs
Houston
Texas 77090

Raintree Designs Inc
979 Third Avenue
New York
NY 10022

Scalamandre
37-24 24th Street
Long Island City
NY 11101

F Schumacher & Co
939 Third Avenue
New York
NY 10022

Van Luit
200 Garden City Plaza
Garden City
NY 11530

Garden furniture and conservatories

Cassidy Bros, Forge Inc
US Route 1
Rowley
Massachusetts 01969

Country Casual
17317 Germantown Road
Germantown
Maryland 20874

Fergusons Cut Glass Works
4292 Pearl Road
Cleveland
Ohio 44109

G Krug & Son Inc
415 W Saratoga Street
Baltimore
Maryland 21201

Park Place
2251 Wisconsin Avenue NW
Washington DC 20007

Robinson Iron Corporation
PO Box 1119
Alexander City
Alabama 35010

AUSTRALIA
Fireplaces

Adelaide Mantlepiece
95 Port Road
Queenstown
Adelaide
South Australia

Agnews
215 Swan Street
Richmond
Melbourne
Victoria

Amazing Grates
398 Lygon Street
Brunswick
Melbourne
Victoria

Antique Firegrates
635 Canterbury Road
Surrey Hills
Melbourne
Victoria

Antique Fireplace Restoration
77 Victoria
St Rozelle
Sydney

Blaze Fireplaces
557 Church
Parramatta

Classic Fireplaces Pty Ltd
12 Sherbourne Road
Briar Hill
Melbourne
Victoria

Colonial Fireplaces
127 Musgrave Road
Geeburg
Brisbane
Queensland

The Fabulous Fireplace
12 Williams Street
Lilydale
Melbourne
Victoria

Fireplace Surrounds
10 Collingwood Street
Osbourne Park
Perth
Western Australia

Mr Stoves
Car Oxley/Allardyce Street
Gracevill
Brisbane
Queensland

Period Fire Surrounds
18 Ferguson Street
Underwood
Brisbane
Queensland

The Pot Belly Stove Co
1138 Burwood Highway
Fern Tree Gully
Melbourne
Victoria

Town & Country Fireplaces
Beecroft
Sydney

The Victorian Marble
Fireplace Co
Hyde Park
Adelaide
South Australia

The Wood & Coal Heating
Advisory Service
231 Bulwer Street
Perth
Western Australia

Glass

Astor Glass Industries
154 Hum Highway
Lansvale
NSW 2166

Bevelite Glass Pty Ltd
3/14 Anvil Road
Seven Hills
NSW 2147

Castlead Works
129 Boundary Road
Peakhurst
NSW 2210

Creative Stained Glass &
Lead Line Designs (1974)
624 Beaufort Street
Mt Lawley
WA 6050

Dowell Australia Ltd
PO Box 244
Preston
Victoria 3072

Glassform
Level 6
51 Queen Street
Melbourne
Victoria 3000

Nielsen & Moller Pty Ltd
PO Box 289
Caringbah
NSW 2229

Oliver-Davey Glass Co
PO Box 238
Noble Partk
Victoria 3174

Seraphic
PO Box 110
Welland
SA 5007

Tiles

The Olde English Tile Factory
73-79 Parramatta Road
Camperdown
NSW 2050

Classic Ceramics
25 Balmain Road
Leichhardt
NSW 2040

Classic Ceramics
93 Queenbridge Street
South Melbourne
Victoria 3205

Classic Ceramics
84 Annerley Road
Woolloongabba
Queensland 4102

Classic Tiles
41 North Terrace
Adelaide
SA 5000

Crosby Tiles
46 Hector Street
Osbourne Park
WE 6017

Graham's Tile Centre
561 Botany Road
Waterloo
NSW 2017

Mingarelli Tiles
11 Nelson Street
Moorabbin
Victoria 3189

Selective Tile Centre
658 Botany Road
Alexandria
NSW 2015

Signorino Ceramics
847 Sydney Road
Brunswick
Victoria 3056

The Tile Centre
287 Main Road
Glenorchy
Tasmania 7010

FRANCE

Ironwork/Staircases

Ets Ch. Schmidt
15 Passage de Main d'Or
75011 Paris

Sercomet
Tel (1) 64 07 19 19

J F Escaliers
108 bd Voltaire
Paris 75011

J F Escaliers
1 chemin de Rispet
Rte de Launaguet
Toulouse 31200

F V L
17 Place du Maupas
F45130 Meung-sur-Loire

Salvage

Recherche
Materiaux anciens pour
restauration et decoration
Tel:16 86 60 12 41

BSL Renovation
32 rue Sambre et Meuse
75010 Paris

SG Construction
28 rue de Montlignon
95390 Saint-Prix

Corema
35 quai du Pre-Long
77400 Lagney

Conservatories

CVR
32 V Route de Niort
85200 Fontenay-le-Comte

Amdega (Aluverre)
30 rue du General Leclerc
Oncy-sur-Ecole
91490 Milly-la-Foret

Atelier 2B
5 et 13 rue Lacharriere
75011 Paris

Pacema
80 avenue du General-de-Gaulle
94550 Chevilly-Larue

Poterie de la Madeleine
Tornac
30140 Anduze

SMF
107 rue Veron
94140 Alfortville

Stoves & Fireplaces

Ets Kalachauf
2 rue Max-Bruchet
74000 Annecy

Cheminees Philippe
Avenue Kennedy
BP 26
62400 Bethune

Franco-Belge
BP
59660 Merville

Michel Boidron
136 Avenue du Medoc
33320 Eysines

Carrieres du Boulonnais
Ferques
62250 Ferques

Carrieres de Etrochy
Ste-Colombe
21400 Sainte-Colombe-sur-
Seine

Gauthier Marbrerie
2-4 rue des Dremeaux
71400
Autun

Marbe du Condado France
Kestastel BP 8
67260 Kestastel

Carpentry

Menuiserie 'Lamarck'
158 rue Lamarck
Paris 18e

SARL Doliger
Artisan Escalieteur
3 rue des Manneliers
59800 Lille

Fireplaces

Michael Boidron
136 Avenue du Medoc
33320 Eysines

Carrieres du Boulonnais
Ferques
62250 Ferques

Carrieres d'Etrochey
Ste-Colombe/Seine
21400 Sainte-Colombe-sur-
Seine

Del Bana
S.A.R.L
BP 42
11300 Limoux

Gauthier Marbrerie
2-4 rue des Dremeaux
71400 Autun

Isocheminee
93 Route Pluguffan
29000 Quimper

Lardit-Bernad
Seviognacq Meyracq

Marbe du Condado France
Kestastel BP8
67260 Kestastel

GERMANY
Fireplaces

Openfire-ROSSLER-Kamine
GmbH
Behringstr 1-3
D-6072 Dreieich-Offenthal

Erwin Koppe GmbH + Co KG
D-8489 Eschenback

Honniges & Holzheuer
D-3394
LaNGELSHEIM 2

KABE-werk Betonfertigtelle
GmbH
Lammerspieler Str 105
D-6052 Muhlheim

Schniedel GmbH & Co
POB 500565
D-Munchen 50

HOLLAND

De Etna BV
Postbus 15
7070 AA Ulft

Siersmeedwerk Charles Sol
BV
Postbus 224
5600 AE Eindhoven

Home Fire BV
Landaasweg 8
3931 GA Woudenberg

Firma Fire Masters
Tarweland 12
3833 VR Leusden

Hercules BV
Postbus 24
5327 ZG Hapert

Barbas Alternative
Verwarming BV
Hallenstraat 15c
5531 AB Bladel

BVL Ringlever (Dovre)
Postbus 11
4140 AA Leerdam

Jos Harm BV
Vijzelgracht 29-31
1017 HN Amsterdam

AShoot Natuursteen BV
Postbus 37
7000 AA Doetinchem

Remy Openhaarden
Insdustrie
Postbus 101
5520 AC Eersel

INDEX

Select Bibliography

Steven Adams, *The Arts & Crafts Movement*
(Chartwell Books, New Jersey, 1987)
Helena Barrett and John Phillips, *Suburban Style: The British Home,
1840-1960* (Macdonald Orbis, London, 1987)
Isabella Beeton, *The Book of Household Management* (London, 1869)
William T. Comstock, *Victorian Domestic Architectural Plans and
Details* (facsimile of 1881 edition, Dover Publications,
New York, 1987)
The Crystal Palace Exhibition Illustrated Catalogue (facsimile of 1851
edition, Dover Publications, New York, 1970) Ralph Dutton,
The Victorian Home (Batsford, London, 1954) Charles Eastlake, *Hints
on Household Taste* (Longmans, Green & Co., London, 1878)
*Floyd, Wells & Co.: Authentic Victorian Stoves, Heaters, Ranges,
etc.* (facsimile of c.1898 catalogue, Dover Publications,
New York, 1988)
Mary Gilliatt, *Period Style* (Conran Octopus, London, 1990)
Robin Guild, *The Victorian House Book* (Rizzoli, New York, 1989)
Bea Howe, *Antiques from the Victorian Home*
(Batsford, London, 1973)
Alan Johnson, *How to Restore and Improve Your Victorian House*
(David & Charles, Devon, 1984)
Robert Kerr, *The Gentleman's House* (John Murray, London, 1864)
Allison Kyle Leopold, *Victorian Splendour: Recreating America's
19th-Century Interiors* (Stewart, Tabori & Chang, New York, 1986)
Matthew Lloyd and Janet Blackmore, *Glass for a Beautiful Home*
(Merehurst, London, 1988)
Judith and Martin Miller, *Period Style* (Mitchell Beazley,
London, 1989)
*Mott's Illustrated Catalog of Victorian Plumbing Fixtures for
Bathrooms and Kitchens* (facsimile of 1888 edition,
Dover Publications, New York, 1987)
Stefan Muthesius, *The English Terraced House* (Yale University Press,
London, 1985)
Katherine Seppings, *Fireplaces for a Beautiful Home*
(Merehurst, London, 198)
*The Victorian Design Book: A Complete Guide to Victorian House
Trim* (facsimile of 1904 edition, Lee Valley Tools Ltd, Ontario, 1984)
Peter Thornton, *Authentic Decor: The Domestic Interior* 1620-
1920 (Weidenfeld, London, 1985)
Aymer Vallance, *The Life and Work of William Morris*

Acknowledgments

Picture Credits
(l) left, (r) right, (t) top, (b) bottom,

Pictures for Print 6, 10, 11, 14, 15, 18, 19(t)(r), 22(b)(r), 23, 26, 27(l)(r), 30, 31(t), 34, 35, 38, 39, 42, 43, 46, 47, 50, 51, 54, 55, 58, 59, 62, 63, 67, 71, 74, 75(r), 79(t), 82, 86, 87, 90, 94, 95, 99, 103(t), 106(b), 119(b), 122(l), 126, 127, 130, 134, 135(t), 138, 139, 150(r), 154, 155, 158, 159, 162, 163, 167(t) Linda Osband 27(t) Billy Carter 19(l), 22(t) Kirsty Mclaren 70 Osborne & Little 75(l), 146(b), 147, 151 Locker & Riley 79(b), 83 Adrian Sankey 78 London Door Company 66(tl) 102(r) Mark Wilkinson Designs 107(t) BC Sanitan 114, 123 Pipe Dreams 115, 118, 119(t), 122(r), Astonleigh Studio 131 Cohen & Pearce 150(l) Robinson & Cornish 98, 102(l), 103 (b)Bracken Books 142, 143, 170 Lighting Designs 146(t) Templar Lighting 162(r) Roy Smith & Son 166(l), 167(b) End of Day Lighting 166 Town & Country Conservatories 174, 175, 178, 179

Photography
Kirsty McLaren 30(tr), 31(b), 38(l), 63, 67(l), 86(r), 90(l), 94, 95, 99, 106(b), 122(l), 126, 134(t), 155, 158, 159
Kevin Mallet 62, 74(b), 82, 90(r), 91(t), 119(b), 127, 134(b), 135(t), 138, 139, 154, 162(l)
Billy Carter 19(l), 22(t)
Other specially commissioned photography through Pictures for Print.